DYNAMITE, TREASON & PLOT

DYNAMITE, TREASON & PLOT

TERRORISM IN VICTORIAN & EDWARDIAN LONDON

SIMON WEBB

First published 2012

The History Press
The Mill, Brimscombe Port
Stroud, Gloucestershire, GL5 2QG
www.thehistorypress.co.uk

British Library Cataloguing in Publication Data.
A catalogue record for this book is available from the British Library.

ISBN 978 0 7524 6378 0

Typesetting and origination by The History Press
Manufacturing managed by Jellyfish Print Solutions Ltd
Printed in India

CONTENTS

	Introduction	7
1	The Roots of Modern Terrorism	11
2	The Anarchist Terror	20
3	The Clerkenwell Outrage	39
4	The First Modern Terrorist Campaign	61
5	Fighting Back: the Political Police in Britain	76
6	The Tottenham Outrage	86
7	The Houndsditch Murders and the Battle of Stepney	96
8	Three Trials	110
9	The India House	122
10	The Terrorists of the Suffragette Movement	130
Appendix 1	A Walk through Radical Clerkenwell	142
Appendix 2	In the Footsteps of Peter the Painter	147
	Epilogue	150
	Bibliography	152
	Index	154

INTRODUCTION

There is in this country a widespread, but wholly mistaken, perception that terrorism in Britain is a relatively new phenomenon, dating back no further than the IRA bombing campaigns of the mid-1970s. Nothing could be further from the truth. In fact, taking any random twenty or thirty year period over the last couple of centuries will reveal terrorist activity in Britain, focused in most cases upon the capital. The IRA were not the first to realise that one bomb in London is worth ten in the provinces. Terrorism has been an intermittent feature of life here since at least the mid-Victorian era. The bomb explosions on the underground which took place on 7 July 2005 were not the first attacks of this sort to be made on London tube trains. As early as 1883, a series of terrorist bombs exploded in the tunnels of the underground and the first person to be killed in such an attack died not in 2005, but in 1897. The worst loss of life in a terrorist attack in London prior to the 7/7 attacks took place not, as one would expect, during the IRA bombing campaign of the 1970s and 1980s, but as long ago as 1867, when twelve people were killed by an explosion in Clerkenwell.

Many of the features of everyday life that we vaguely suppose to be manifestations of a modern emergency have actually been around for well over a century. In the closing years of Victoria's reign people were writing to the newspapers complaining about having to queue up in order to have their bags searched before being allowed into museums. Bodyguards for politicians, security measures for public buildings, letter bombs and suicide bombers were all around before the First World War.

Today, many people in Britain are concerned about what they see as dangerous subversives and potential terrorists embedded in alien communities which have established themselves in the larger British cities. In the past, as now, such fears were often inextricably bound up with unease about immigration and fears that foreigners were taking jobs away from the people who were born in this country. There is talk of 'Londanistan', the idea that a separate community of potentially dangerous Muslim outsiders has made its home in the capital and lives next to but separately from us. Such fears are not new. They are simply the latest manifestation of a very British phenomenon. Over the last couple of centuries, there have been periodic scares of this sort, featuring the same anxieties and demands for precisely similar action on the part of the authorities. Emergency legislation to tackle extremism or combat terrorism, the suspension of habeas corpus, identity cards, new controls over immigration – all these have been recurring themes since at least the 1860s.

The focus of fears about terrorism has varied from decade to decade. At one time it was Indians and Irishmen, at others women or Jews. Frequently, uneasiness about terrorism is bound up with a general feeling amongst ordinary citizens that there is a crisis involving immigration, combined with rapid and unwelcome changes in society. Such fears seem as fresh as today's newspaper headlines, with our own era's obsession with Islam and worries about uncontrolled immigration as a result of our 'porous' borders. Many of the incidents at which we shall be looking have an eerily modern feel about them. An armed robbery by asylum seekers in a London suburb goes disastrously wrong and a policeman is shot dead. Two years later, three police officers are shot dead by another group of foreign terrorists; the army is called in to help when a siege subsequently develops, with which the police are unable to deal. Bombs planted at the Tower of London and Scotland Yard, explosions on the underground, calls for the routine arming of the police in order to deal with the unprecedented threat to security – all these events took place over a hundred years ago. Yet, they have somehow been forgotten. Each generation feels that the threats of this sort facing them are uniquely terrible and far more dangerous than any seen previously in this country.

The latest menace of this kind with which we in Britain are allegedly confronted – that of Islamic terrorists being sheltered in closed communities, seemingly having little in common with the rest of us – is nothing new. In this book we shall try to place such concerns in context and look at the broader historical picture. We shall be looking at many of the familiar figures from the modern debates on immigration and terrorism. Eastern Europeans who are taking jobs away from those born in this country, asylum seekers who end up shooting at our unarmed police officers, radicalised Asian youths who have fallen under the influence of preachers of hatred – all these were regularly featured in the newspapers of a hundred years ago.

Consider the exchanges in Parliament with a Home Secretary, in this case Winston Churchill, trying desperately to defend the government's record on immigration. This was in the aftermath of the use of troops to tackle foreign terrorists in London who had shot dead three unarmed police officers. On 8 February 1911 the Home Secretary faced some hard questioning in the House of Commons. The exchanges between Winston Churchill and various MPs could have been lifted straight from a debate this week in Parliament. An MP called Croft called upon the Home Secretary to tell the House how many foreigners had entered the country over the course of the last year. The answer was an astonishing 600,000 in 1910 alone; over half a million in just one year. Even by today's standards, this was an incredibly large influx. Nevertheless, Churchill then tried to calm fears by insisting that the net increase in foreigners had to be balanced against the number also leaving the country over the same period.

Another MP then asked the Home Secretary if it was true that the crime rate had fallen during the years towards the end of the nineteenth century and was now rising due to the presence of large numbers of foreign criminals. Churchill denied this. Another question dealt with people trafficking. The Home Secretary mentioned that this had become a problem, as large groups of people were being smuggled into the country, but that he felt this was now under control. There was also a suggestion that foreigners were entering the country to obtain medical treatment.

It is hard not to come to the conclusion that Winston Churchill, back in 1911, was facing precisely the same kinds of searching questions about terrorism and its possible connection with immigration and asylum seekers as present-day home secretaries regularly find themselves having to deal with. In the spring of 1911, new controls on immigration were promised in the form of an amendment to the 1905 Aliens Act.

Another curious resonance with the past is the way in which famous London landmarks like St Paul's Cathedral, Big Ben and Westminster Abbey have supposedly been in the sights of terrorists since the 1860s. The clock tower of the palace of Westminster known popularly as Big Ben, for instance, is apparently under threat today from terrorists. Those who carried out the 7/7 bombings had, we are told, plans to attack Big Ben and, in December 2010, the police announced the uncovering of another plot involving this internationally known tourist attraction. The image of Big Ben may be seen as symbol of 'Britishness' or social and political stability. As such, the fear of its destruction has cropped up regularly over the years. In Plate 2 we see how this anxiety was expressed in the 1890s. In the aftermath of the Irish attack on Clerkenwell Prison in 1867, rumours circulated that both Big Ben and St Paul's Cathedral would be blown up by terrorists and, as we shall see, St Paul's Cathedral and Westminster Abbey had bombs planted in them a year before the First World War.

To make sense of the history of terrorism in this country, it will first be necessary to look at the special attraction that this country held for refugees and asylum seekers during the reign of Queen Victoria.

1

THE ROOTS OF MODERN
TERRORISM

The origin of terrorism, as it is currently practised throughout the modern world, is to be found in late nineteenth-century London. This is not say that terrorism started in London or that before 1890 there was no such thing as terrorism; rather that the very idea of terrorism before that time was formless and vague. It was in London during the 1870s and 1880s that the theoretical basis for terrorist activity was formulated and it came to be seen as a legitimate form of political action for those who had no other recourse in their struggle against a repressive or authoritarian state. Why should it have been in London that these theories first began circulating? The reason is simple. In many European countries, activists, agitators and subversives were constantly hounded by the police and imprisoned or driven into exile.

The British were generally happy for anybody to come to their country and, so long as they lived respectably and did not make a nuisance of themselves, they could say or write what they pleased. There were, at least until 1905, no restrictions at all on immigration in this country. Once they were here, there were no identity cards, demands for papers, harassment by secret police, arbitrary imprisonment or the threat of deportation. Under such conditions, foreign intellectuals, writers and left-wing thinkers found that they had the leisure to think and freedom to publish their thoughts whenever they felt like it, within certain limits. We shall see later what these limits were and what the consequences were for those who exceeded them.

So it was that London became the refuge for political thinkers, particularly those on the left, who needed peace and quiet in order to think through their ideas, draw up manifestos, write books and, in some cases, plan revolutions. Karl Marx naturally gravitated to London in 1849 and remained there until his death thirty-three years later. Lenin too found a safe haven in London, where he lived and worked for some time while publishing his revolutionary newspaper *Iskra*, the Spark. Stalin and Trotsky too spent time in London, plotting revolution. Other foreign-born radicals who settled in the capital are less well known. Johann Most, the German anarchist, and Prince Peter Kropotkin, a Russian, are among those whose names may not be immediately familiar to most people. Their writings and speeches in London, however, laid the foundations for every modern terrorist campaign from the IRA to Al-Qaeda.

Before we go any further, it might be a good idea to ask ourselves just what we mean by the word 'terrorism'. The British Government defines terrorism as 'the use or threat, for the purpose of advancing a political, religious or ideological course of action, of serious violence against any person or property'. This is sufficiently vague as to include everything from crowds of student demonstrators all the way up to the invasion of Iraq. The usually accepted view of terrorism is that it is limited to acts of violence carried out by a non-governmental agency. In order to qualify as terrorism, such acts really need to be of such a nature as to cause, or be likely to cause, serious injury or death. In practice, this means the use of guns and explosives.

Now there have always been groups of people prepared to advance their cause by setting off explosions and shooting people. This practice certainly did not originate during Victoria's reign. There is a sharp difference, though, between the practice of terrorism before this time and its later use. The most chilling aspect of terrorist campaigns as they are currently conducted is that any one of us may become a victim. This creates a general fear or apprehension, which is, of course, precisely the aim of modern-day acts of terrorism. It is this, the essentially random nature of the injuries and deaths produced, which was unknown before the mid-nineteenth century.

What was called 'terrorism' throughout much of history has really consisted of targeted attacks on particular groups or individuals. These might be pogroms directed against Jews or Catholics, or perhaps the assassination of government leaders. In many cases, it was a matter of pride for those carrying out these attacks that nobody but the specific target of their attack should suffer any injury or harm. The perpetrators of such actions have been described as 'good terrorists'. This type of terrorist was epitomised by Ivan Kalyayev. A member of a revolutionary group in Russia during the rule of the tsars, Kalyayev decided to assassinate Grand Duke Sergei

Alexandrovitch, General-Governor of Moscow and uncle of the tsar. Kalyayev prepared a bomb and waited for the Grand Duke's carriage to pass. When it did, he saw to his horror that the duke's wife was also in the carriage, along with a group of young nephews. He refused to kill any innocent victims and so abandoned his plan. He later threw a bomb at the duke, killing him, when he was travelling alone.

Principled behaviour of alleged terrorists was very common in nineteenth-century Russia. These people, members of groups such as the *Narodnaya Volya* (People's Will), were almost fanatically careful not to harm any bystanders when carrying out assassinations. This tactic, the so-called 'blow at the centre', proved useless in the long run. There was no shortage of new men prepared to step into the shoes of some murdered police chief or city governor. The ordinary citizens remained apathetic, viewing the assassinations and executions almost as some species of private quarrel that didn't really concern them. It was this indifference of the general public that caused some political thinkers to decide that a more effective way of using bombs would be to aim them at the general population. This, if anything, would be guaranteed to shake them out of their complacency. These theoreticians were aided by scientific discoveries being made at that time in the field of chemistry.

In 1847 Ascanio Sobrero, an Italian, was studying chemistry at Turin University under the tutorship of a Professor Pelouze. Sobrero was experimenting with a mixture of sulphuric and nitric acid, which he had combined with glycerine. He was actually trying to devise new medicines when he made the mistake of heating this deadly mixture in a test tube. Fortunately, the test tube contained only a small quantity of the ingredients, because as soon as it was held over a flame, there was a loud crack and the test tube exploded. Sobrero was injured by fragments of glass, but he had really got off very lightly indeed. The oily liquid which he had produced was nitroglycerine.

Sobrero was shaken by the experience, but continued his work with this dangerous new compound. He fed some to a dog, which promptly died. While dissecting the unfortunate creature's body though, Ascanio Sobrero made a very important discovery. The blood vessels in the dog's heart were hugely dilated. It at once occurred to him that here could be a remedy for angina and other problems of the circulatory system. Today, nitroglycerine is still the most widely used treatment for circulatory problems involving the heart.

Sobrero realised at once that there was another and more dangerous side to this new drug. In larger quantities, it had the potential to be used as a weapon of war. The only explosive known at that time was gunpowder: a compound of charcoal, sulphur and saltpetre which had been in use for a thousand years or so. However, as a matter of fact, gunpowder is not really an explosive at all. It is simply a substance which will burn very fast indeed. It only explodes if it can be enclosed in a container such as a gun barrel or bomb casing.

If one fills a saucer with gunpowder and then touches it with a red hot needle there will be no explosion. The powder will flare up very quickly and if you are not careful, you might end up singeing your eyebrows. Try the same trick with a saucer of nitroglycerine and you will probably blow off your hand. It will explode at once, whether or not it is enclosed in a container. It is, in the jargon of the trade, a high explosive; in contrast to gunpowder, which is a low explosive.

The new explosive was in great demand, but it suffered from one quite literally fatal defect. It was so sensitive that it was liable to explode if banged, splashed, dropped or even shaken too hard. It also deteriorated over time into unstable compounds, which could explode spontaneously without any warning. A fortune awaited the man or woman who found a way to make the new compound stable enough for general commercial use. This fortune was duly made by Alfred Nobel from Sweden, who was, coincidentally, another former pupil of Professor Pelouze of Turin. Nobel found a way of absorbing nitroglycerine into a type of clay called Kieselguhr, so that it became safe to handle. In 1867 he patented this process and the resulting product became known by the trademark of 'dynamite'.

Nitroglycerine revolutionised warfare in the nineteenth century through a range of new explosives, but its potential for conventional armies was not the end of the story. Gunpowder was never really a convenient substance for producing bombs or grenades; it is simply not powerful enough. It is also very hard to manufacture to the right quality, unless you happen to be running a factory. A few sticks of dynamite, though, made the perfect bomb to throw. Even if one had no access to commercial explosives, it was possible, although hideously dangerous, to synthesise nitroglycerine at home out of the basic ingredients of sulphuric and nitric acid, added to glycerine in the right proportions. Dynamite became known as 'the poor man's artillery'. It was the perfect tool for what was becoming known as 'propaganda by the deed'.

The expression 'propaganda by the deed' originated with the anarchist movement that was active in the 1880s in both Europe and North America. The idea was simple. Instead of writing long, convoluted pamphlets and tracts that no ordinary person would read anyway, why not capture the attention of the public by acts of terrorism? Many people had become accustomed to the idea of a president or police chief being assassinated and so to seize their interest it was necessary to make these terrorist acts outrageous and a threat to ordinary people. Thus was born the classic strategy of urban terrorism that we see today. Every modern terrorist group follows the pattern first set out by anarchists living and writing in London around 1880.

In 1881 Johann Most, a Bavarian anarchist who had been imprisoned in his own country and subsequently sought asylum in Britain, published a booklet called *The Philosophy of the Bomb*. In it, he formulated the strategy which terrorists follow today. First, it is necessary to attract the attention of the public by acts of violence that are likely to affect them personally. It is no good simply killing some soldier or policeman. As we saw in Russia, after a while people lose interest in such activities. This type of action, propaganda by the deed, would awaken the population to political issues in a way that mere words could never do. Once violence of this sort became frequent enough, the next stage would be reached. The state would react with repression, aimed at the bombers and assassins but likely to affect the general public. This would have the effect of alienating ordinary people and making them hostile to towards the government and their agents, the army and police. This cycle, acts of terrorism by individuals and reprisals by the state, would escalate into a spiral of violence. Ordinary citizens would inevitably be drawn into this conflict. The endgame would see the masses angry and disillusioned with the forces of law and order and driven into the arms of the terrorists, whom they would have finally realised had the same aims and values as they did themselves. All this was very well in theory, but in practice it often did not work out according to plan. This was especially so in Britain, a country long noted for its tolerance towards minorities and dissidents.

The whole practical aim of all terrorism in the twenty-first century is firmly based upon the ideas expressed by Most, Kropotkin and Errico Malatesta, an Italian anarchist who was also living in London during the 1880s. It has, however, proved notoriously hard to provoke the state in this country into savage repression of the kind necessary to kick-start a revolution or popular uprising. This is because instead of relying upon all the paraphernalia of dictatorships – the identity cards, secret police, arrest and imprisonment without trial and suchlike – the British have always relied upon a far simpler method for combating extremism. It is, almost invariably, done not by the apparatus of the totalitarian state, but by the simple use of informers and double agents.

This has been the tradition in this country since long before the nineteenth century, but it was with the beginning of the Industrial Revolution that the paid informer really came into his own. The problem is that there is often a very fine line dividing the informer from the agent provocateur; between the man or woman who just tells the authorities what is going on and the person who actively encourages and incites others to illegal activities. This is a line that has been regularly crossed in this country and never more so than during the attempt to deal with the European terrorists who found refuge here during the closing years of Queen Victoria's reign.

Just as the police today seem to be able to nip the majority of terrorist conspiracies in the bud, so too did their nineteenth century counterparts. Informers ran anarchist magazines, rose to important positions in the Irish Fenian movement and seemed to have a hand in most of the plots which were uncovered. In many cases, it looked suspiciously as though they were themselves the instigators of the plots that they revealed to their police handlers. The problem with using paid informers is, of course, that they need to keep coming up with dangerous conspiracies in order to justify their very existence. Some double agents of this sort rely upon the money which they make from their activities and so of course a thriving terrorist network is vital for their livelihood. No police force is going to bother recruiting and financing agents who are just keeping an eye on men who write books or give speeches. It is essential that threats to public order and safety are regularly discovered. This all too often results in the actual creation of such threats that otherwise would not have existed. This theme, that of the agent who actually precipitates terrorism where none would otherwise have occurred, is explored in detail in two books published only a few months apart in 1907 and 1908.

In the next chapter we shall look at how the threat from terrorism was reflected in popular literature around the turn of the century, but I wish to examine first *The Secret Agent*, by Joseph Conrad, and *The Man who was Thursday*, by G.K. Chesterton. The central theme of both these works is the role of police agents in encouraging terrorist activity in Britain. As this is something of a *leitmotif* in police actions against terrorist groups in this country, right up to the present day, I think it is worth looking in detail at some of the ideas behind this way of combating the threat of terrorism.

The Secret Agent is loosely based upon an actual incident, when an anarchist attempting to plant a bomb at the Greenwich Observatory was killed when his bomb detonated prematurely. In the book, the double agent uses his brother-in-law as a dupe to carry the bomb to its intended target. The brother-in-law of the man actually killed in the attempted bombing of Greenwich Observatory was in real life a police agent who was also the editor of the anarchist magazine *Commonweal*. The suspicion was that he had actually persuaded his impressionable young brother-in-law to carry out the attack on Greenwich, exactly as Conrad describes in the fictionalised account given in *The Secret Agent*. This book is fascinating for the exposition that it gives of the role of the informer and how he could be manipulated by unscrupulous paymasters into working to their agenda.

Mr Vladimir, an official at the Russian embassy, explains to Verloc, the eponymous secret agent, why it is imperative that a bomb attack take place in London. Verloc is a member of an anarchist gang and Vladimir wishes him to stage what we would today call a 'spectacular' in order that Britain should be 'brought in line', as he calls it. At the time that the novel is set, the British habit of allowing anybody to come to their country and promulgate any political view was beginning to irritate other European countries. As Vladimir says: 'England lags. This country is absurd with its sentimental regard for individual liberty ... England must be brought into line. The imbecile bourgeoisie of this country make themselves the accomplices of the very people whose aim is to drive them out of their houses to starve in ditches.'

Vladimir proposes that the double agent instigates a completely mad and pointless terrorist explosion at Greenwich Observatory. This would have the effect of causing the British Government to 'come into line' and crack down on anarchism in the same way that other European countries were doing at that time. This sort of repression was, of course, precisely what the terrorists themselves were trying to provoke. In other words, the aims of the terrorists and also those who were opposed to them often actually coincided. Both sought the same end. We will see this time and again in the cases at which we shall be looking. It is frequently impossible to distinguish those plots that were actually started by double agents and informers from others where they simply observed and passed on information. Like the secret agent Verloc in Conrad's novel, these men relied upon a constant stream of conspiracies and outrages for their living. It is hard not to draw comparisons with police and MI5 activity against Islamic terrorists today. Those whom they pay are under pressure to justify their existence and it is possible that some of the plots of which we hear would not have come into existence except for the actions of the informers themselves.

In G.K. Chesterton's novel *The Man who was Thursday*, this close identification of the hunter with the prey is taken to its logical and absurd conclusion. The protagonist, whose code name is Thursday, is a police agent who is trying to infiltrate the central committee of the anarchists. He eventually manages to do so, only to find that all the other members of this group are, like him, police agents. In other words, the anarchist movement is being run and co-ordinated by the police themselves. This idea comes pretty close to the truth in some counter-terrorist work and is not as farcical as it might at first appear. The extreme left-wing magazine *Commonweal*, mentioned above, had not one but two police informers on its editorial board.

Of course, it is not only informers who need to keep uncovering new conspiracies in order to justify their existence. The same applies to police departments and intelligence agencies tackling subversion. If there are no revolutionaries or terrorists in town, then these people would be out of a job. This gives such units an interest in the continued existence of a terrorist threat. In Victorian London, it was hard to tell which of the plots and conspiracies were being detected and deterred by the police and which they had started themselves. There is even a strong suspicion that the police were involved in a plan to assassinate Queen Victoria and the entire Cabinet.

So how did the British tackle extremism during the Victorian and Edwardian periods? None of the extreme measures advocated by those who regarded anarchism and Fenianism as deadly threats to the nation were ever adopted. Just as in our own day, milder and more restrained methods were generally found to be effective. We have seen in the last decade or so that attempts have been made to introduce identity cards and detention without trial in order to deal with the unprecedented threat that the nation faces. The same tools were demanded by those fighting terrorism a century ago. Then, as now, common sense prevailed.

The best way of dealing with the threat of terrorism has always been not to play into the hands of the terrorists by passing ferocious new laws, but rather to use existing legislation to tackle the situation. Johann Most was surely one of the most bloodthirsty and hot-headed anarchists living in London in the 1880s, but he was not persecuted by the police or driven into exile. He was watched, though, and when he overstepped the mark, the ordinary law was found to be quite sufficient to deal with him.

When Most settled in London, he started a newspaper called *Freiheit*, which advocated revolution and individual acts of resistance to the state. Some of what Most wrote in this paper sailed pretty close to the wind and, even today, one might run into difficulties if one started encouraging readers to 'shoot, burn, poison, stab and bomb' as Most did. Following Tsar Alexander II's assassination on 1 March 1881, Most allowed himself to get carried away and published a fulsome congratulation to the tsar's killers. He headed the piece with 'Triumph, Triumph' and went on to call for the murder of one monarch every month. This really was a bit much, even in a liberal democracy like the UK, and Johann Most found himself in the dock, charged with seditious libel. Today, we would probably describe this sort of thing as 'glorifying terrorism'. He was sent to prison for sixteen months and, when he was released, decided to move to the USA.

Most's story shows very clearly how the British have, in the past, and indeed still do, meet the danger of terrorist agitators. Not by ferocious punishments and the midnight knock on the door, but rather by giving such people plenty of leeway and then using the existing law if they stray too far in the direction of inciting violence.

It is time now to examine in detail some of the terrorist campaigns that were conducted from the 1860s onwards. To begin with, we will be looking at an international conspiracy whose members embraced an ideology and belief system quite alien to those in Western Europe or America. They loathed our very way of life and wished to smash it to pieces. These people were utterly merciless and quite prepared to sacrifice their own lives to the cause in which they believed. They planted bombs in European cities, heedless of the casualties they might cause. They even bombed the London Underground. The Special Branch in this country was constantly discovering new plots and raiding bomb factories set up by these people, who were associated with the communities of foreigners who seemed to have taken root in our big cities – a consequence of our porous borders. I am, of course, referring not to Islamic terrorists such as Al-Qaeda, but to the anarchist movement that flourished at the end of the nineteenth century.

2

THE ANARCHIST TERROR

The final years of the nineteenth century saw the emergence of a frightening new phenomenon: an international terrorist organisation whose members subscribed to a strange and almost incomprehensible ideology. Their aim was nothing less than the destruction of the way of life that was enjoyed by the citizens of the liberal democracies of Western Europe. These ruthless men and women despised those democracies and were quite prepared to lay down their lives for their cause. Their favoured means of attacking the societies, which they viewed as being essentially decadent and deserving of annihilation, was by random bomb attacks in crowded public places such as streets, railways stations and theatres. This was not a matter of some small group of nationalists seeking freedom from a colonial oppressor. Rather, it was dedicated individuals linked by a common belief who so hated our way of life that they were prepared to kill others and sacrifice their own lives in a furious and determined attempt to bring down the fabric of our society.

Many readers will at this point perhaps be experiencing an unsettling feeling of déjà vu. When we learn that these fanatical terrorists were being sheltered in communities of asylum seekers who had made their homes in this country and that there was increasing concern at the ease with which such people could enter the country and settle here, many of us will probably see disturbing parallels with our own concerns over asylum seekers and Islamic terrorists.

The motivation behind the wave of terrorism which struck Europe and to a lesser extent the United States as the century drew to a close was not Islam but anarchism. This was an ideology which held that the existing institutions of society, from marriage to the stock exchange, were hopelessly corrupt and needed to be swept away. Their argument against the democracies of Western Europe was not whether the party in office should be Conservatives or Liberals, or if this or that law should be amended or reformed; they wished to bring down the entire edifice and start again from scratch. Like the radical Muslims, who feel that our way of life here in the West is rotten and perverted, so too did the anarchists hope to clear away everything for which Western European civilisation apparently stood. Needless to say, such wholesale condemnation of their lifestyle did little to endear the anarchists to ordinary citizens.

Throughout Europe at this time, a series of attacks were being mounted by anarchists, many of whom came from Eastern Europe and Russia. Their bombs targeted anybody whom they viewed as being wealthy, powerful or even middle class, and explosions took place in a variety of public places. They were also responsible for a number of political assassinations, including those of the President of France in 1894 and the American President William McKinley in 1901. The aim was to throw respectable citizens into a panic; a goal that they certainly achieved. The anarchists, together with some socialists, wished to destroy bourgeois society and sought to do so by striking at the leaders and institutions of the parliamentary democracies of Europe, and also by random terror against that class whom they blamed most for the state of modern society: the bourgeoisie or propertied middle classes. As one anarchist said at the time, 'I shall not strike an innocent if I strike the first bourgeois I meet!' Such acts of terrorism were known as 'Propaganda by the Deed'.

The anarchists believed rightly that bombs and assassinations would draw far more attention to their cause than mere words. They would also, it was hoped, provoke violence from the police and army, which would in turn reveal to citizens the essential nature of state power; that it was predicated upon force and maintained at gunpoint. The theoretical basis for this new wave of terror was first expounded in London, a city that was soon to become known throughout world as the greatest safe haven for terrorists and revolutionaries.

The feeling in Europe at the time was that the traditional Western European way of life was under siege. Most European countries had controls on immigration and periodically Russian anarchists and other refugees were simply expelled from one country or another. Britain alone had no control over the movement of foreigners in and out of the country. The inevitable result was that as France, Spain and Italy cracked down in turn upon foreign-born subversives, those deported gravitated naturally to this country. At the same time many Jews were fleeing Russia and they too headed for what was seen as the most easygoing and welcoming country in Europe. London was spoken of in consequence in some European countries as 'the Cesspool of the Universe'. According to the police in Berlin, 'The whole of European revolutionary agitation is directed from London'. It is instructive to compare this with the front page of the *Daily Telegraph* on 26 April 2011, which proclaims in a large, front-page banner headline: 'London: hub of al-Qaeda's global terrorism network'.

It is almost impossible today to realise just how uneasy the presence of these strangers made many British citizens feel. They often spoke strange and unfamiliar languages; not the French or German with which many educated English speakers had at least a nodding acquaintance, but more commonly Yiddish, Polish or Russian. They lived in ghettos, ate peculiar food, dressed differently and, most alarmingly of all, their communities provided hiding places for terrorists and turned the capital city into a launch pad for attacks in other countries. Since they were being driven from country to country because of their race, ethnicity or political beliefs, the great majority of these people fell into the category of what we would today call 'asylum seekers'. All this will be very familiar to those used to hearing talk of 'Londanistan' and the development of separate communities, comprising largely of asylum seekers who follow disturbing and fundamentally un-English ideologies. The parallels with the modern anxiety about Islamic terrorists are quite uncanny. Just as today we worry about the Islamophobia, which is thought to be growing among some people who fear the influx of immigrants from Africa and the Middle East, so too in the 1890s was there concern about the anti-Semitism provoked by the increasing number of Jews entering the country from Russia. From the very beginning of this unprecedented wave of immigration, anarchism and socialism were firmly connected in the popular mind with the large number of Jews coming here.

It is quite true that many anarchists were Jews, but this clearly does not mean that all, or even most, Jews were anarchists. The situation then precisely mirrored that which we face today, when most terrorists in Britain are Muslims. Thoughtful people are of course exceedingly careful to avoid falling into the trap of assuming from this that a natural corollary is that most Muslims are terrorists. However, for the ordinary working-class person in London at that time, the Jews became inextricably associated with strange and dangerous ideas; they were seen as a clear threat to our own way of life. There were even rumours in 1888 that Jack the Ripper was a Jewish anarchist.

The fears of ordinary people about this influx of dangerous foreigners were reflected in the popular culture of the late nineteenth and early twentieth centuries. In 1893, for example, at the height of the panic, E. Douglas Fawcett published a novel called *Hartman the Anarchist or the Doom of the Great City*. The great city was, of course, London and the book featured a lurid illustration of Big Ben being destroyed by a huge explosion. It was not by chance that the villain was given a Jewish-sounding name. Other novels published around this time dealt with similar themes of mass murder and destruction. In one, anthrax was deliberately spread in London by foreign terrorists and another involves the construction of a 'dirty bomb', which kills the people in the city while leaving its buildings unharmed. In fact, the threat of an anthrax attack was actually regarded by the Special Branch in 1894 as being quite credible and by no means merely the stuff of cheap thrillers. H.G. Wells used the idea of mass murder by anarchists as the theme for his short story *The Stolen Bacillus*, published in 1895. In this story, an anarchist steals a vial of cholera germs from a laboratory and plans to use them to contaminate London's water supply. On the way to the reservoir, though, the tube breaks and he realises that he has become infected with the disease himself. He decides instead to wander through the city and spread the germs himself in what is, essentially, a suicide attack. This notion, that a fanatical terrorist might infect himself with a disease such as smallpox and spread it through a city in this way, is a current nightmare of the security services.

Perhaps the most eerily prescient of such popular fiction was the novel *Emperor of the Air*, which was published in 1910, after the anarchist scare had begun to subside a little. In this book, by George Glendon, terrorists use aircraft to attack America. One illustration shows an aircraft loaded with explosives about to crash into a New York skyscraper. The scene of devastation in New York, with buildings destroyed and people fleeing in panic, is irresistibly reminiscent of the 11 September attacks in 2001. One of the most famous thrillers ever written in this country, *The Thirty-Nine Steps*, first published in 1915, centres around a plot by Jewish anarchists to provoke a world war.

The first bomb plot connected with the anarchist movement in England was disrupted by Scotland Yard before it really got off the ground. The conspiracy that was revealed struck great fear into the hearts of ordinary people in London. Just as today, when converts to Islam have been implicated in some of the worst of the attempted terrorist outrages, so too with the anarchists. There were signs that Englishmen were being converted to their cause and joining them in planning bomb attacks on the capital.

In 1889, a socialist club was started in the Staffordshire town of Walsall in the Midlands. The secretary was a man called Joseph Deakin and the members of the club met regularly to discuss the new political ideas that were appearing on the Continent. It was all fairly harmless until 1891, when a new member arrived in Walsall and joined the club. Frederick Charles came from Sheffield, where he was active in socialist and anarchist circles. No sooner had he settled in Walsall than he confided to Joseph Deakin that he was in touch with anarchists both in London and France. The two men invited a French anarchist called Victor Cailes to Walsall and then, on the recommendation of another Frenchman, Auguste Coulon, contact was made with a third man in London, an activist by the name of Jean Battola.

At this point things become a little murky. Deakin and Charles visited London and Battola visited Walsall, and somewhere along the line a plan was hatched to construct a bomb. This was to be made with a metal casing, somewhat like an enormous hand grenade. Two other members of the socialist club, John Westley and William Ditchfield, were enlisted to help cast the casing of this bomb, although it later appeared that neither man actually knew that it was a bomb at all. What nobody realised was that Auguste Coulon was in fact a police agent, acting directly on the instructions of Detective Inspector William Melville of Scotland Yard's Special Branch.

We meet here for the first time the informer or agent provocateur. Detective Inspector Melville, who was Auguste Coulon's 'handler', to use the modern intelligence term, had been a founding member of the Special Irish Branch when it was started at Scotland Yard in 1882. The year after the Walsall plot was uncovered he was promoted to superintendent in charge of the Special Branch. After he took charge of the Special Branch, he fired a sergeant called McIntyre. McIntyre went to the newspapers and made the sensational allegation that the entire Walsall plot was actually Melville's brainchild. He claimed that Auguste Coulon had set everything in motion on Melville's instruction because the police were anxious to get some hard evidence against anarchists. Files released many years later suggested that there may well have been something to this. At the very least, the police appeared to have been far too closely involved in the affair.

The same accusation of police involvement was made in the magazine *Commonweal*. A member of the magazine's editorial board, Henry Samuels, was a police informer himself and, by an interesting coincidence, a friend of Auguste Coulon. Nor was he the only police informer on *Commonweal's* editorial board; Charles Mowbray, who also wrote for the magazine, was in the pay of the Special Branch. Another real-life example of the infiltration of revolutionary movements by the police, suggesting that the superficially absurd thesis of *The Man who was Thursday* may not have been so very wide of the mark.

On 6 January 1892, Joseph Deakin caught a train to London, intending to meet up with Battola. He was arrested, carrying parts of the bomb, after the train arrived at Euston station. Over the next few days Cailes, Battola, Westley and Ditchfield were also picked up, and in April 1892 all five men appeared at the Stafford Assizes, accused of conspiring to cause an explosion. In his defence, Deakin claimed that he thought the bomb was to be used in an attempt on the life of Tsar Alexander III of Russia. Westley and Ditchfield, who clearly had no idea what they had become involved in, were acquitted. Deakin received a fairly lenient sentence of five years, while Charles, Cailes and Battola were each sent to prison for ten years.

Meanwhile in Europe, the anarchists were having more success with their activities. On 7 November 1893, two bombs were detonated at the Liceo Opera House in Barcelona. A total of twenty-nine people were killed, nine of them women, while many others were blinded or lost limbs in the attack. As a result, the constitution of Catalonia was suspended and emergency powers were imposed upon the whole province. Many anarchists fled from Barcelona to France and then from there to England.

English newspapers were quick to announce that the Barcelona bombing had been planned in London. The *Evening Star* claimed:

> There is ample proof that the plot which culminated in the Barcelona tragedy was planned in London. It now appears that the police are in possession of a document found amongst the papers of the Walsall Anarchists when they were captured in London in 1892. The MS. is headed 'A Fete at the Opera,' the whole of which is devoted to the description of the blowing up of an English theatre while full of people.

The writer went on to say that the British Government was partly to blame for the Barcelona bombing because they were complacent about the large number of foreign subversives entering the country. London was being used as a haven for the terrorists and it was high time to crack down.

Three weeks after the Barcelona bombing, Auguste Vaillent, a French anarchist, threw a nail bomb from the public gallery into the Chamber of Deputies in Paris, the French equivalent of the House of Commons. Twenty men were injured, although nobody was killed. Despite this, Vaillent was sentenced to death. Ten days later, on 19 December, the question of immigration and the number of terrorists sheltering in this country was raised in Parliament by J. Cumming Macdona, MP for Southwark. He asked Sir Edward Grey, Under Secretary of State for Foreign Affairs:

> I beg to ask the Under Secretary of State for Foreign Affairs if he is aware that Signor Amilcari Cipriani, the notorious Italian socialist, is stated to have left Paris for London; whether M. Raynal, Minister of the Interior in the French Government, has prepared a list of persons to be expelled, comprising about 200 names of foreign anarchists or socialists residing in France, mostly Italians, Germans, and Russians of most violent and reckless tendencies, to be immediately expelled from that country; and whether, in view of the fact that persons expelled from France prefer coming to London, as easier of access and affording them greater freedom of action, he will state what steps the Government propose taking to prohibit these dangerous foreigners landing upon our shores?

Sir Edward was dismissive of the question, saying, 'I have no information as to the statements in the first two paragraphs, while the subject dealt with in the third does not come under the cognisance of the Foreign Office.'

Nevertheless, there was increasing uneasiness and a belief that England was becoming a soft touch, the favoured destination of choice for rootless foreigners, among whom there were a considerable number of terrorists and preachers of hatred. *Plus ca change, plus c'est la meme chose* (the more things change, the more things stay the same).

As 1893 drew to a close, there was a definite feeling that things could not continue in the same way and that sooner or later the government would be obliged to take action to stem the tide of immigrants believed to be entering the country. Alongside fears of terrorism were complaints that British jobs were under threat from the cheap labour provided by the foreigners, and also that they were responsible for a disproportionate amount of crime and disorder in the areas where they settled.

The Walsall bomb plot had been foiled, but the danger was not over. On 15 February 1894, an attempt was made to blow up the Royal Observatory at Greenwich. This failed only because the attack resulted in what has become known today as an 'own goal'. In other words, the bomber succeeded in blowing himself up, rather than his intended target.

On 3 February 1894, Auguste Vaillent went to the guillotine for his bomb attack on the Chamber of Deputies. His last words were a chilling war cry: 'Death to the Bourgeoisie!' It was perhaps inevitable that an attempt would be made to avenge his death. On the evening of 12 February, a little over a week after Vaillent's execution, Emile Henry, a 22-year-old Frenchman, threw a bomb into the Cafe Terminus at the Gare St Lazare railway station in Paris. One woman was killed and another twenty people were injured. After his arrest, it emerged that this was not the first bomb attack in which young Henry had been involved. A little over a year earlier, on 8 November 1892, he had planted a powerful device at the offices of the Carmaux Mining Company. This had not exploded and the police had taken the bomb to their headquarters in order to deal with it. It went off in an office at the police station, killing five officers.

There is another strange parallel here between modern-day Islamic terrorists and the anarchists of the late nineteenth century: neither group seemed particularly worried about sacrificing their own lives. When Vaillent hurled his bomb into the Chamber of Deputies, he made no effort to escape and must have known that he faced the guillotine for the attack. The same applies to Emile Henry and many other anarchist terrorists and assassins of the time. Just as modern-day suicide bombers are quite prepared to lose their lives in a cause in which they believe, so too were the anarchists. This indifference to one's own life and death is very chilling to most people and, at the time of the anarchist campaigns, it caused many to speculate that these bloodthirsty fanatics must be insane.

Three days after Emile Henry's attack on the Cafe Terminus, the last two members of staff working at the Royal Observatory in Greenwich Park that day were preparing to go home. It was a quarter to five in the afternoon and all the other workers had left. Mr Thackeray and Mr Hollis had been completing a tricky piece of mathematical calculation relating to astronomical observations. They were just getting ready to leave the building when they heard a loud report, something like a clap of thunder. On going outside to investigate, they saw a park keeper and a group of schoolboys running towards a point on the path which led up the hill to the observatory. They went to see what was happening and were appalled to see a horribly muti-lated body lying on the ground. Splashes of blood and fragments of the man's body, including a 2in length of bone, were found up to 60 yards from the scene of the explosion. Later, more than fifty pieces of flesh and bone would be collected from the surrounding area.

The dead man was a 26-year-old Frenchman called Martial Bourdin. He had lodgings in Fitzroy Street and that afternoon had caught a tram from Westminster which took him to Greenwich Park. The conduc-tor had observed that he had with him a parcel, of which he seemed to take particular care. Bourdin did well to take care of his parcel, because later investigations showed that he had been carrying a large can full of nitroglycerine. Nitroglycerine is perhaps the most dangerous and unstable explosive imaginable. It is an oily liquid which will explode if jogged or splashed. As we saw in a previous chapter, it was by finding a substance that would absorb nitroglycerine and make it safe to handle and transport, that Alfred Nobel made his fortune. Dynamite is essentially nothing more than nitroglycerine which has been absorbed by kieselguhr clay. The attraction of nitroglycerine for terrorists is that it can be fairly easily synthesised from just sulphuric acid, nitric acid and glycerine. Unless, however, you know precisely what you are doing, you are likely to end up killing yourself in the process. At the best of times, nitroglycerine is a horribly sensitive and unstable liquid which will explode with devastating force if you so much as blink at it.

A large sum of money was found on Bourdin's body and the police con-cluded that he had been planning to return to France after carrying out the attack on the Royal Observatory. It seemed a strange target for a bomb attack. The only advantage would appear to be that it was high up on a hill and any explosion would presumably have been seen and heard for miles around. The observatory was also the symbolic heart of modern timekeep-ing and, in a sense, science.

In Bourdin's pocket was discovered a membership card for an anarchist club based in a side street off the Tottenham Court Road called the *Club Autonomie*, along with thirteen gold sovereigns and identification which led police to his home address. That a tailor's assistant like Bourdin should have had £13 in his pocket, a large sum of money in those days, was a suspicious circumstance in itself. It led the police to suppose that he intended to flee the country as soon as he had planted the bomb he was carrying. Also in his pocket was a tram ticket to the Woolwich Arsenal. According to witnesses, who had been travelling on the same tram as the dead man, he had seemed extremely nervous, constantly peering around behind him. He jumped off the tram at Greenwich rather abruptly, as though on an impulse. On reflection, it seemed likely to the police that he thought he was being followed and that the choice of the Royal Observatory as a target for the bomb was made on the spur of the moment. There's no doubt that the government's military gun and explosive-making factories at Woolwich would have made a far more logical and prestigious target for a terrorist attack than the Greenwich Observatory.

When Bourdin's lodgings were searched, police discovered a bomb-making factory. There were large bottles of sulphuric acid and bags of various chemicals which could be combined to make explosives. In addition to this, there were also stacks of political leaflets as well as instructions in French for making time bombs. The membership card for the *Club Autonomie* aroused a good deal of interest among the officers of the Special Branch to whom it was shown. Joseph Deakin, the Walsall bomb maker, was actually on his way to this very location when he was arrested at Euston station. Scotland Yard set up an ingenious plan to investigate the place. The *Club Autonomie* was a small drinking den at No 6 Windmill Street, a little to the north of Oxford Street. The police, led by Detective Inspector Melville, arrived early in the morning a couple of days after the Greenwich explosion and took over the place. Then they simply waited. As members began to arrive in the afternoon, each man was admitted by a plainclothes officer and immediately arrested. All the members who came that day were searched and held incommunicado, so no warning was given to anybody else planning to come there. The membership book was also examined and found to contain a number of very familiar names. Emile Henry, for example, the young man who had hurled a bomb at the Gare St Lazare railway station in Paris, had visited the club a few weeks before he was arrested. Altogether, over eighty people were arrested following the raid on the *Club Autonomie*. No explosives were found there, although it was fairly plain that the place was being used as a regular meeting place for foreign anarchists.

Bourdin's funeral, a week after his death, was a very disorderly affair. Charles Darling, the MP for Deptford, tried to get the funeral banned, even raising the matter in Parliament. He argued that since Bourdin had brought about his own death by his actions, he should be treated as a suicide and not buried in a graveyard at all. There was a great deal of popular anger against anarchists in particular and foreigners in general, and others shared Darling's view of the matter. One can imagine how a funeral procession in London today for a suicide bomber might provoke ordinary Londoners, and their reactions would probably be pretty much the same as those which Bourdin's funeral cortege encountered. There were cries of 'Get back to your own country!' and 'Long live England!' The police had already warned Bourdin's friends and fellow anarchists that they would be unwise to make too much of a procession for the funeral, but they decided to risk it anyway.

Unsurprisingly, the whole thing degenerated into a riot. As not infrequently happens today, the police found themselves playing piggy-in-the-middle, caught between a small group of unpopular foreign activists and a large crowd of angry Londoners. Mounted police were called in to control the crowds and the hearse eventually reached St Pancras cemetery. Hundreds of police fought to keep order as the coffin was lowered into the ground, and some of those heckling and calling out the more extreme xenophobic slogans were arrested, as was an anarchist who tried to make a speech at the graveside, in direct defiance of police instructions.

After the funeral, the angry mob showed no signs of dispersing and made its way to Windmill Street, where the *Club Autonomie* was besieged. Stones were thrown and the windows smashed, while a few people leaving and entering the place were roughed up and their clothes torn. After an hour or so, the crowd eventually dispersed peacefully.

In the years following the Greenwich bomb, stories began to circulate to the effect that the whole incident had been a carefully staged provocation, perhaps orchestrated by the police. The aim, it was suggested, was to provide a pretext for cracking down on anarchists living in London. Some weight was given to this theory by the undisputed fact that Martial Bourdin's brother-in-law was Henry Samuel, editor of *Commonweal*. He was a police informer in regular contact with Inspector William Melville. The idea was mooted that Bourdin was no more than a dupe and that his brother-in-law had been behind the whole enterprise. It was also suggested that Melville himself was somehow aware of what was planned. Over a century later, we shall probably never now know the truth of the matter.

This then was England's first taste of the terrorism which was sweeping the Continent. Although London had experienced bombs before during the 1860s and 1880s, this was something else entirely. The Fenian dynamiters, much as they were hated and despised, at least had as their motive a clear and understandable aim: the establishment of an independent Ireland. They posed no threat to society as it was presently constituted and no desire to change it either. They simply wanted the British to withdraw from their country. The anarchists, on the other hand, were trying to destroy civilisation itself, or so it must have seemed to many at the time. Like some Islamists today, they felt that Western civilisation was decedent and morally bankrupt. They wished to smash it to pieces and on the ruins erect what they saw as a more just and equitable society. They were opposed to our way of life and determined to attack at any time or place in order to spread terror and, they hoped, bring about the collapse of the present order.

The explosion at Greenwich was immortalised in fiction by Joseph Conrad in his 1907 novel *The Secret Agent*. Conrad, himself a Polish immigrant whose real name was Korzeniowski, wrote in detail of the strange world of the anarchist conspirators. Although fiction, many believe that Conrad's novel provides a startlingly authentic insight into the émigré community of the 1890s which harboured such men as Martial Bourdin.

The police actions following the explosion at Greenwich will sound familiar to anybody in England today. The first step was to make life difficult for any suspected foreign terrorists living in the capital. This was done in a number of ways. One was to round up any such people and photograph them. These photographs and the descriptions of the men were then circulated to employers, with the advice that these individuals should not be given a job. The aim of this was to make foreign anarchists so hard up that they would wish to leave the country of their own accord. In some cases, this tactic was successful. Another thing that the police in London did was to keep a watch for any subversives who were actually wanted for crimes in their own country. They could then be picked up and deported. This did not always work smoothly, as we shall see in the case of Errico Malatesta. With Théodule Meunier though, the scheme worked brilliantly.

Meunier was wanted in France for bombings which had taken place after the arrest of another well-known anarchist bomber, Ravachol. He had fled to London, and Superintendent Melville, by this time head of the Special Branch, arrested him in person as he was about to leave the country. He was later extradited to France, where he stood trial. He was sentenced to life imprisonment on a French penal colony at Cayenne, where he died fourteen years later.

Unlike the Fenians with their American connections and the anarchists in Europe, who were able to obtain commercial explosives and construct their bombs with dynamite, the anarchists in this country were forced to manufacture their own explosives from scratch. Most of us will have seen police anti-terrorist advertisements showing dustbins crammed with empty containers of bleach or a garage with a huge stockpile of hydrogen peroxide. This is, of course, because the suicide bombers who struck at the London Underground on 7 July 2005 had used home-made explosives, which they had managed to synthesise from fairly innocuous substances. Just as the police today have circulated warnings to chemists, so too did the Special Branch of Scotland Yard back in 1894. Rather than ask them to take particular note of anybody buying large amounts of hydrogen peroxide, though, it was sales of concentrated sulphuric acid that they were asked to keep an eye on, particularly if those attempting to buy large amounts had foreign accents – an early example of suspect profiling.

So it was that a few weeks after the death of Bourdin, Mr Herbert Pretlock, who was an assistant at the Taylor's Drug Company shop at 66 High Holborn, was at once suspicious when a young man with a very strong Italian accent entered his shop and asked to buy 2 pints of concentrated sulphuric acid. A week before, two foreigners had entered an ironmongers yard in Blackfriars Road and told the manager that they wished to construct a curious piece of machinery. This was to consist of a length of iron piping with two plates to seal off the ends. One of the plates was to be fitted with a nipple, in order that some liquid could run in or out of the apparatus. No sooner had the two men left a deposit with him than the owner of the yard went to the nearby police station to report what seemed to him to be a very suspicious business indeed.

From the very beginning, therefore, this plot was compromised. For a foreigner to buy a quart of sulphuric acid in the weeks following the Greenwich bombing was likely to excite the same kind of unfavourable interest as would an Arab attempting to buy a gallon of hydrogen peroxide following the 7 July attacks in London. However, just as they do today, the police watched and waited, hoping that they would be able to catch any others who might be implicated in the conspiracy. It was not until the middle of April, two weeks after they had become aware of the plot, that the police struck.

On 14 April, the young Italian who had purchased the iron piping went to the shop to collect it. On his instructions, metal plates had been fixed to the ends of the pipe and he seemed quite satisfied with the work. When he left the shop, he was obviously not aware that four of the passers-by in the busy street were plainclothes detectives of the Special Branch. They trailed the young man, getting onto a bus with him and then all got off in

Farringdon Road. It was not until he began fiddling with the heavy piece of iron that they pounced. Eighteen-year-old Francis Polti was arrested and his room searched. There the police found bottles of sulphuric acid and also a quantity of home-made explosives. He was charged with having in his possession and control certain explosive substances, with intent to endanger life and property. His accomplice, the man who had first accompanied him to the ironmongers, was traced and also arrested on the same charge. His name was Guiseppe Farnara and he was a 44-year-old Italian.

The trial of the two men took place at the Old Bailey on 30 April 1894. It was fairly clear by then that the object of the conspiracy had been to plant a bomb at the Stock Exchange, that symbol of capitalism. Farnara, who spoke no English at all, did little to endear himself to the court. On being asked how he pleaded, he answered through an interpreter, 'I wanted to kill the capitalists!' On being asked if he understood the charge against him, he replied, 'Yes, I plead guilty. I had the intention to blow up the capitalists, and all the middle classes.' This was not a tactful thing to announce when standing in the dock at the Old Bailey. The police were careful to call enough witnesses to prove the case against the two men without any sort of doubt. The result was that both were found guilty; the jury retiring for only four minutes before returning with their verdicts. Polti received a sentence of ten years, while his companion was given twice as long. One cannot help but suspect that Farnara's avowed desire to blow up all the middle classes might have had the effect of alienating the judge and removing entirely any sympathy he might have felt for the man.

Six weeks after Polti and Farnara's trial, another onetime member of the *Club Autonomie*, an Italian anarchist called Sante Geronimo Caserio, assassinated President Carnot of France by stabbing him to death. It was beginning to look to other European countries as though all the terrorist plots being hatched had their origins in London. Representations were made to the British Government, urging them to be harsher with the refugees who were making their home in London.

One member of the *Club Autonomie* was very lucky in his jury when he came up for trial at the Old Bailey charged with having explosive substances. Fritz Brall and his wife came to London from Germany in 1893. He was a cabinetmaker and also an anarchist. His home in Tottenham Court Road became a haunt of European anarchists who were living in London at that time. Not unnaturally, he eventually came to the attention of the Special Branch. When they raided Brall's home, it seemed at once as though they had uncovered a bomb factory. Containers of both sulphuric and nitric acids (the basic ingredients of nitroglycerine), cartridges, fulminate of mercury and batteries which looked as though they were part of a firing mechanism were found. There was also a huge amount of anarchist propaganda and, intriguingly, a leaflet called 'Scientific Revolutionary Warfare', which was in effect a bomb-making manual. At Brall's trial on 25 June, Inspector Sweeney of the Special Branch said, 'This pamphlet was a very remarkable work and the mere possession of it unexplained should be made as serious offence as the possession of explosive materials.'

Brall's neighbours had evidently had a lot to put up with. Elizabeth Fox told the court how she had heard a terrific explosion from Brall's flat, which was beneath hers. She went on to say: 'The first explosion I heard was just before Christmas, and it was a fortnight before I heard any more – I cannot say when the last one was, but they went on for about a month or six weeks – I think there were seven or eight explosions in that time.'

Another witness called by the police, Mary Ann Charlotte Foster, was a frequent visitor at Elizabeth Fox's home. She too had heard the explosions. Fritz Brall had a ready explanation for these alarming noises: he had been trying to clear his chimney by throwing fireworks up it. This is not quite as far fetched as it sounds. Calling in a chimney sweep was quite expensive and many poorer people did rely upon this method of clearing blockages from their flues. Brall's employer was called as a witness and testified that some of the chemicals found in his home were actually used in cabinet making. He singled out the battery and sulphuric acid as the sort of things that were useful in clearing verdigris from brass.

By the time he began summing up, it seemed that even the judge was beginning to have doubts about the strength of the case. The jury had no such doubts, retiring for only fifteen minutes before returning to acquit Fritz Brall of running a bomb factory. It rather looks, reading the transcript of the case over a century later, that the police assumed that any foreign anarchist was more likely than not to be up to no good.

There were no more incidents in London itself until the middle of summer. On the night of 14 August, there was an explosion in south London. The post office in New Cross Road was almost destroyed by the fire which followed the bomb's detonation. Although witnesses described a man seen running from the scene, no arrests were made. A note was found at the scene. Written in French, it mentioned Bourdin and other anarchists, ending in a call to arms for the working classes. Two more post offices were attacked in the same way in the next few weeks, but it was to be over two years before the culprit was brought to justice.

In Deptford, a working-class area of south London, there was a club where anarchists met every Sunday night to discuss politics. The police kept a watchful eye upon this place and its Sunday-night meetings were usually attended by an officer in plain clothes. On the night of 24 January 1897, Police Constable Michael Walsh had the job of going along and listening to the speeches of the mainly foreign anarchists who were trying to convert English working men to their cause. On this occasion, conversation turned to the explosion at the Licea theatre, which took place in 1893. One of the men present, a 36-year-old Englishman called Rollo Richards, seemed to know so much about explosives that PC Walsh made a note of what he was saying and details of his appearance. For instance, the topic under debate was nitroglycerine and Rollo Richards was apparently very familiar with its preparation and use.

The next day, PC Walsh contacted Scotland Yard and passed on the information he had gathered the previous day. The result was that, on 6 February, the police raided Richards' home. When they knocked on the door and announced that they had a warrant to search the premises, Richards made a bolt for the kitchen, but was quickly overpowered. There was a violent struggle and he shouted, 'My God! Had I known you were coming I would have had a chisel and gouged your eyes out.' A quick search revealed that the house was a bomb factory. Richards himself was English, but had many connections with French and Italian anarchists. He had spent some time in an asylum and the suggestion was made that he had been put up to the attacks on the post offices by his comrades.

At his trial for arson on 5 April 1897, extensive evidence was given against Rollo Richards. It was obvious that he had been manufacturing bombs and planting at least some of them in London. The impression was that he was a little weak in the head and that other, cleverer men had made use of him. The verdict was never in doubt and on conviction he was sent to prison for seven years. This was a relatively light sentence, an indication of the general feeling that he had been used as a dupe. Nobody expected his former comrades to seek revenge for his conviction and imprisonment.

The reaction to Richards' trial came three weeks later in what was perhaps the most serious attack of the whole campaign in London. It took place at ten past seven in the evening of Monday 27 April. A Metropolitan Line underground train, crowded with people heading home from work, had just arrived at Aldersgate station in central London. As the doors opened, there was a tremendous explosion in one of the first-class carriages. The carriage where the explosion occurred was practically destroyed and the station was soon filled with the screams and moans of the injured. The force of the blast shattered the glass roof of the station and the crowds stampeding away from the scene were showered with broken glass. Pieces of twisted metal from the carriage scythed across the platform, severing limbs. Only one person was actually killed, which at the time seemed nothing short of miraculous. However, in the light of modern experiences, such as the 7 July tube bombings in 2005, it is fairly easy to see why casualties were so much lighter in 1897.

The force of an explosion is fairly swiftly dissipated if it meets no obstruction. In a large, open station such as Aldersgate, the main force went upward, wrecking the glass roof 50ft above the platform. By contrast, the 7 July bombs exploded in tunnels. The force of the explosions there was thus contained and reflected back into the carriages by the walls of the tunnel. Most of the casualties at Aldersgate suffered superficial cuts, bruises and burns, although a number of people lost arms and legs. And, of course, one man lost his life. Harry Pitts was a 36-year-old manual worker, who was originally from Devon but had settled in Tottenham, north London. He was standing right next to the bomb when it went off and must have died instantly.

It was not immediately apparent that the explosion had been caused by a bomb; the first suspicion was that a gas main had blown up. The day after the explosion, Colonel Majendie, the Chief Government Inspector of Explosives, visited Aldersgate and examined the wreckage of carriage No 93. It did not take him long to see that the explosion had taken place inside the carriage and that it could only have been caused by a powerful bomb. There were no leads at all though as to who had planted the device and although the coroner's jury at the inquest into Harry Pitt's death brought in a verdict of 'Wilful murder by person or persons unknown', nobody was ever arrested for the crime.

A bizarre memento of this crime is to be found in the London Transport Museum in Covent Garden. Fragments of metal from carriage No 93 were collected as souvenirs and one piece was sculpted into a miniature replica of the carriage, which was even painted realistically in the livery of the Metropolitan Line. This grotesque little model was then mounted on to, of all unlikely things, an ornamental inkwell. For some years a clerk at the railway had this peculiar little item on his desk, though it is now on display in the museum.

In 1898 a secret conference was held in Rome which was attended by representatives of twenty-one governments, including those of Germany, Switzerland, Italy, France, Denmark and Spain. The aim of this anti-anarchist meeting was to thrash out an international agreement for dealing with the scourge of terrorism. A number of countries had already passed laws specifically aimed at anarchism, but this was an attempt to forge a unified European approach to the problem. Although nothing definite was agreed at this meeting, it set the stage for the establishment of a Europe-wide intelligence-sharing agreement; a project which later became formalised as Interpol. Meanwhile, the assassinations and other terrorist acts continued.

In the same year that the conference in Rome was held, Empress Elizabeth of Austria was murdered by an anarchist. Between 1894 and 1912, no fewer than eight monarchs or heads of state were assassinated by anarchists in Europe and America. No other terrorist organisation, before or since, has come anywhere near to carrying out quite so many ruthless murders of national leaders. In 1898 Kaiser Wilhelm of Germany refused to visit Egypt because he was afraid of being assassinated by Italian anarchists based in neighbouring Libya.

In 1900, the Prince of Wales, soon to become Edward VII, was passing through Belgium on the way to Denmark. While he and his wife were sitting in their carriage and waiting for the train to leave from the Gare du Nord station in Brussels, a 16-year-old anarchist called Sipido rushed up to the window and fired a revolver twice at the Prince of Wales. Incredibly, both shots missed not only the prince but also everybody else in the compartment. The young man, an Italian, was seized and taken into custody. His subsequent trial almost provoked a diplomatic incident with Britain. This was because the court ruled that, at 16, he was too young to been fully responsible for his actions. He was acquitted and simply released. Three months later, King Umberto of Italy became another victim of the anarchist terror, dying at the hands of an assassin.

Perhaps the most famous anarchist assassination of all took place the following year when a Polish anarchist by the name of Leon Czolgsz shot and killed the President of America, William McKinley. This action sent shock waves around the world and was a clear signal that the anarchists were not yet a spent force.

Meanwhile in Britain, the political violence seemed to have more or less petered out. Large numbers of asylum seekers were still flooding into the country from Russia, Poland and the Ukraine, but the fears concerning this mass immigration had become almost exclusively concerned with the social and economic effects. The general public felt that the main danger from unrestricted immigration lay in the increasing unemployment and lower wages faced by British workers as they faced competition from the huge new pool of cheap foreign labour; a familiar enough concern in this country a century later. These anxieties were to lead in 1905 to the passing of the Aliens Act, the first attempt in British history to limit and control immigration.

However, if anybody thought that the threat of violence in England had really diminished, the first decade of the twentieth century would soon prove them spectacularly wrong. Indeed, the half-hearted, bumbling efforts of the anarchists of the 1890s were soon to be put to shame by the deadly actions of some of the professional revolutionaries who were now making their homes in the capital. Those first few peaceful years of the new century were merely the lull before the storm.

Before we look at how the situation developed in the Edwardian era, we must first go back a little and look at what happened in the middle of Queen Victoria's reign. The anarchists were not the first to introduce terrorism and political violence to England. That distinction belongs to another group of outsiders to mainstream society, the Irish. Their community shared some of the features which we have seen in the Eastern Europeans who came to live in this country at the end of the nineteenth century. They were mistrusted, regarded with suspicion and their presence was generally viewed as being undesirable. Many of them entered this country as asylum seekers, survivors of one of the worst famines ever to strike Europe. Some of them also waged war upon their host society, a fact that caused ordinary people to view every member of their community with a certain degree of distrust.

We shall begin by looking at the events that took place in 1867, the year in which the worst terrorist atrocity staged in the capital prior to the attacks of 7 July 2005 took place. This attack signalled in some ways the beginning of the world's first modern terrorist campaign.

3

THE CLERKENWELL OUTRAGE

The crowd had been gathering all night and by eight o'clock on the morning of 26 May 1868 it had become immense, occupying a large area to the west of St Paul's Cathedral. In all the narrow streets surrounding Newgate Prison, people stood crammed shoulder to shoulder. Windows and rooftops above them were packed to capacity, the well-to-do having paid up to 20 guineas each for the privilege of gaining a grandstand view of the proceedings. Some of them had come from as far away as Birmingham and Manchester to be spectators at that most gruesome of entertainments: a public execution.

The Industrial Revolution and the dawn of the Age of Reason had done nothing to diminish the English public's appetite for hangings. Indeed, the technological advances of the Victorian age had been harnessed to facilitate the easier attendances of the working classes at these popular events. For the previous fifteen years or so, the newly formed railway companies had been running excursion trains to towns staging the execution of notorious criminals. The executions themselves were boisterous and festive occasions, with even humble apprentice boys traditionally being given the day off work to see the hanging. Soft-drink vendors circulated among the crowd, comic songs were sung, sermons delivered, speeches made and pockets picked. Whole families would camp out overnight to secure an unobstructed view of the scaffold.

However, the execution about to take place that May morning was the last public execution in Britain. Within a few days, the Capital Punishment within Prisons Bill was due to receive the royal assent. From then on, all executions in Britain were to be conducted in private, behind prison walls.

The knowledge that this was to be the last such free entertainment of this sort gave an added piquancy to the occasion and ensured that the crowds would be even greater than usual.

Michael Barrett, who was destined to be the last person publicly executed in Britain, was a 27-year-old Irish labourer. He had been sentenced to death for his part in what had become known as the Clerkenwell Outrage. At the Old Bailey, he had been found guilty of deliberately causing a massive explosion in London a couple of weeks before Christmas 1867, an explosion which had claimed the lives of twelve people and injured over 120 more. Even by today's standards of suicide bombers and car bombs, it had been a 'spectacular' terrorist attack.

In order to understand the crime for which Michael Barrett was to hang that May morning, it will be necessary to look a little at the historical background of this country's dealings with Ireland. Technically, throughout the whole of the nineteenth century, Ireland was as much a part of the United Kingdom as Scotland and Wales. Many Irishmen were violently opposed to British rule in Ireland, though, and from time to time rebellions and uprisings took place, which the British suppressed by the ruthless use of overwhelming military force.

These periodic bloody bouts of guerrilla warfare and the need for the use of British troops to tackle them gave the people in mainland Britain a somewhat jaded view of the Irish. In fact, almost incredibly, for a large part of the nineteenth century the Irish were viewed not so much as a separate nation, but rather as a different race. This was an extraordinary outlook which ultimately provided the British with justification for treating Irish men and women as being less than fully human. It gave rise to an attitude, even among educated English people, somewhat analogous to South Africa in the apartheid days. We were ruling an inferior people who could not really be left to tend their own affairs. Our administration was for their ultimate benefit, although they were ungrateful enough to repay us with regular attacks upon the machinery of our government there. To understand what gave rise to this peculiar point of view, we need to see how Darwin's theory of evolution was misunderstood by many of the intelligentsia in mid-Victorian Britain.

The idea of the existence of separate races and the superiority of some races over others was an article of faith for most people in nineteenth-century England. It seemed self-evidently true that white people were better than black people and that the white race represented a higher stage of development than the black. Sometimes, this sense of superiority was founded upon scripture. The white races were believed to be the descendents of Noah's sons Shem and Japhet, while black people were the children of Ham. As everybody knew, the children of Ham were, according to the Bible, destined to become 'hewers of wood and carriers of water'. The servants, in fact, of the children of Shem. Bible passages such as this provided justification for everything from slavery to the conquest and pacification of new territories in Africa. The publication of *On the Origin of Species* in 1859 allowed some to apply new and apparently scientific ideas to the theory of races.

It had long been accepted that the Irish people were Celts, rather than Anglo-Saxons. To the English, the Anglo-Saxon represented everything which was high and exalted among the various races: the perfect form of the white race, several notches above other types of white, such as the swarthy Latins and other Mediterranean peoples. The Anglo-Saxon was held in as high esteem in Victorian England as the Aryan was to be in Nazi Germany. The Celts, though, were regarded as being a particularly degraded and barbarous subdivision of the white race. Darwin's theories allowed the matter to be placed upon a proper, scientific footing. If it was true that men had evolved from apes, then surely some types of men were closer to the apes than others? Black Africans, for instance, seemed clearly to have had more in common with their simian forebears than the white man. The Celt, as typified by the Irish, was actually a breed closer in ancestry to monkeys than the Anglo-Saxon. Some even tried to prove that the Irish were the 'missing link' between man and ape. This nonsense made perfect sense to the Victorians. Charles Kingsley, the author of that famous children's book *The Water-Babies*, wrote to his sister during a visit to Ireland:

> I am haunted by the human chimpanzees I saw along that hundred miles of horrible country. I don't believe they are our fault. I believe there are not only many more of them than of old, but they are happier, better, more comfortably fed and lodged under our rule than they ever were. But to see white chimpanzees is dreadful; if they were black, one would not feel it so much, but their skins, except where tanned by exposure, are as white as ours.

It was this terrible and skewed perspective which cast those Irish men and women living in England so perfectly for the role of suspect outsiders. Cartoons of the time in magazines such as *Punch* show Irishmen with long jaws and a semi-human, unmistakably ape-like appearance.

Following the failure of the Irish potato crop in 1845 and again in 1846, there was a terrible and widespread famine in Ireland. It is impossible to say how many men, women and children actually starved to death during this time, but what is known is that somewhere in the region of a million Irish people left their own country and immigrated to England and America in the years following the famine. Most of these immigrants were poor and unskilled and they tended to settle in the slums of England's larger cities: Liverpool, Manchester and, of course, London. Many of the men found work as navvies, helping to build the network of railways which was spreading rapidly across the British Isles at that time. They had distinctive accents and some spoke Gaelic among themselves rather than English.

This unprecedented wave of immigration was unsettling and alarming to many English people. As explained above, the Irish were seen as being fairly primitive and brutish, and nobody was especially keen to have them as neighbours or offer them work. This is how they came to be doing the rougher and harder sort of labouring. This tendency for immigrants to take the jobs that the native-born English feel are somehow below them has, of course, also been a feature of the waves of immigrants who arrived here in the latter half of the twentieth century. The new arrivals in the 1840s and 1850s stood out from their neighbours in another way, by their religious observance. In our own time we have seen how terrorism in this country has become associated with an 'alien' religion, Islam. For some people today, the terms 'Muslim' and 'terrorist' fit together as neatly and easily as 'bread and butter' or 'horse and cart'. This tendency to associate dangerous outsiders with strange and unfamiliar religions or ideologies has also been a feature of life in this country for centuries. Immigrants from Russia and Eastern Europe in the late nineteenth and early twentieth centuries followed disturbing ideas such as atheism and socialism; many were also Jews who worshipped in synagogues. In the case of the Irish, their religious difference was an adherence to the Roman Catholic Church.

There had, for at least 300 years, been a powerful sentiment in England against the Roman Catholic Church. For many Anglicans, and also those in other denominations such as the Methodists and Presbyterians, the Roman Church was almost a pagan institution. The fact that the majority of the Irish immigrants followed this religion marked them out, regardless of any other consideration.

There was one more thing that marked the Irish as outsiders. This was their distinct lack of patriotism and in many cases downright opposition to the institution of the monarchy, which was in stark contrast to the average citizen's views. Even among the poorest slum dwellers was by and large to be found a sentimental regard for the queen. Not so with many of the Irish refugees who crowded into the poorer districts of our cities. They had little reason to feel well disposed to the British at the best of times, and seeing huge numbers of their countrymen starving to death and being forced by hunger and poverty to flee Ireland could hardly be expected to make them over fond of the country that they blamed for many of their misfortunes.

So it was that the Irish were, from the very moment they first arrived in this country, already outsiders; men and women to be viewed with fear and dislike. Many of the notices and advertisements of the type that were common in Britain during the 1950s and early 1960s, such as 'Room to let. Sorry, no coloureds', were first used in the mid-nineteenth century against Irish immigrants. They have become known as NINA notices, an acronym formed from the initial letters of the typical formula used: No Irish Need Apply. The result was that, as has happened with other waves of immigrants over the last couple of centuries, the Irish were confined to the poorer areas of Britain's large cities.

Roman Catholicism was not the only strange and unfamiliar creed embraced by many of the Irish of the nineteenth century. Not a few of them were also republicans who rejected the very idea of a monarchy. This idea, which was regarded as being as radical to the point of seditious in Britain, was of course considered perfectly normal in America. Perhaps it is for this reason that the first Irish republican terrorist group was started in that country. In 1858 a secret society was founded by Irish expatriates living in the United States. It was called the Irish Republican Brotherhood and its aim was to free Ireland from British domination. This was to be done in several ways: firstly, by the traditional means of attacks on the British Establishment in Ireland, but also by attacks on British territory overseas and even on the mainland itself. The American Government was fairly tolerant of the activities of the IRB, who were also known as Fenians to most. Several amateurish and ill-fated attempts were made to 'invade' Canada from the USA and a rising was planned in Ireland. This failed when the plans for its execution were accidentally left on a train and found their way to the British authorities in Dublin. It was in England in 1867, though, that events took a particularly tragic turn.

The rising in Ireland had been scheduled to take place in March 1867. Obviously, a large number of weapons would be needed if the British forces were to be defeated. Fenians in Ireland had a few pikes, shotguns and muskets, but nowhere near enough to equip a proper army. It was decided to mount an audacious operation in England in order to acquire sufficient arms and ammunition to furnish the rebels with the means to fight the British army on equal terms. The target of this conspiracy was Chester castle in the north of England. At that time, the castle contained an arsenal of over 10,000 rifles, along with almost a million rounds of ammunition. Only sixty regular soldiers were stationed at Chester castle to guard these weapons. The first part of the Fenians' plan entailed attacking a smaller arsenal of weapons belonging to the Chester Volunteers, a part-time militia who were roughly analogous to the present-day territorial army. Once they were armed, the plan was to storm the castle, seize the weapons of the regular army and then commandeer a train to transport them to Liverpool docks, where they would hijack a ship to take them and their arsenal to Ireland. The rifles would then be distributed to the waiting rebels. This was planned for 11 February 1867.

By any standards, this whole operation looked like an attempt to start something exceedingly close to a war on mainland Britain. Luckily, the authorities in Chester got wind of what was being planned. The rifles of the volunteers were removed to the castle armoury for safekeeping and the garrison was reinforced by regular troops from Manchester. Over a thousand Irishmen were already making their way to Chester by train from surrounding towns, such as Preston, Leeds, Halifax and Manchester. A train containing one of the ringleader of the enterprise, 'Captain' John McCafferty, was shunted into a siding and a train full of heavily armed troops rushed to the city in its place. As word spread that their plot was compromised, this disorganised mob melted away back to their homes. The next day, another 500 soldiers arrived to guard the castle and the entire business more or less petered out. It set the scene, though, for events later that year.

After the failure of the 1867 rising and the fiasco of the Chester castle affair, some of the leadership decided to regroup in England. There were large Irish communities in big cities such as London, Manchester and Liverpool, and the leadership of the IRB felt that these would provide a natural haven for them as they planned the next stage of the struggle to free Ireland. Then, as today, the communities of asylum seekers were viewed as the natural refuge and sphere of operations for terrorists planning to strike at targets in this country. Among the men who fled to England were

Colonel Thomas J. Kelly and Captain Timothy Deasy, both of whom had fought on the Confederate side in the American Civil War. In September 1867, they were in Manchester, trying to raise support for another attempt at driving the British from their homeland.

In the early hours of 11 September 1867, Kelly and Deasy were arrested under the Vagrancy Act on suspicion of preparing to break into a shop. It was only when they were taken back to the police station that the arresting officers realised that they had captured two prominent Fenians. Extreme high security was arranged for their journey from the magistrate's court to Belle Vue Prison. An escort of twelve officers accompanied the locked prison van. Inside the van itself, guarding the prisoners, was Sergeant Charles Brett of the Manchester Constabulary. He and the accompanying guard were armed only with cutlasses. As the van reached the railway arch on Hyde Road, it encountered a large group of armed men. Some were carrying axes and crowbars, but many had pistols. They surrounded the van and held off the police escort at gunpoint. According to the statements of some of the police officers, the assault was led by a man called Richard O'Sullivan-Burke. The intention of the mob was plainly to release Kelly and Deasy. They swarmed over the van, hacking at it with hatchets and hammering at the locked door with rocks and stones. It was at this point that tragedy struck. One of the crowd called to Sergeant Brett, who was guarding the prisoners inside the locked van, to open the door. There were no windows and so to see what was going on he must have tried to peer through the keyhole. At the same moment, somebody fired a revolver at the lock, probably with the intention of blowing it open. Brett fell back dead. The bullet had passed through his eye and into his brain, killing him instantly. One of the prisoners in the van took the keys from his body and opened the door. Kelly and Deasy were soon spirited away and were never recaptured. Sergeant Brett was the first policeman in Manchester to be killed in the course of duty.

The Times carried an editorial a week later which might have been taken from a newspaper commenting on the 2005 attacks on the London Underground. Simply change 'Fenians' to 'Al-Qaeda' and the sentiments are similar to those voiced at the time of 7 July 2005. On 19 September 1867, *The Times* said, 'It is startling to find ourselves face to face with an armed enemy in one of the most important cities in the kingdom. The Fenians have declared war on our institutions and have carried it to the very heart of the country.'

Sergeant Brett's funeral was an occasion for the general public to demonstrate their sympathy for his family and also their detestation for the Fenians. The crowds lined the route of the cortege for over 2 miles.

The authorities reacted with fury to this astonishing crime. It was beginning to look in some quarters as though there were a large number of Irishmen living here who felt no loyalty at all to this country. This was more than a handful of extremists; the raid on Chester had, it will be remembered, been supported by well over a thousand men. The attack on the prison van too involved large numbers of men. Raids were mounted on the Irish community in Manchester and by 28 September twenty-eight men stood in the dock accused of the murder of Charles Brett. Even at the time there was a suspicion that most of those charged with the murder had been picked up more or less at random from among the labourers living in the Manchester slums. Two of the accused were discharged during the preliminary proceedings, leaving twenty-six to stand trial later that year.

There was no evidence at all to suggest that any of the men on trial for their lives had actually fired the fatal shot. Legally, this was not necessary. It was enough for the Crown to prove simply that they had been present at the murder and were participating in the attempts to free Kelly and Deasy from the prison van. At the trial on 28 October it was decided to proceed with the murder charge against only five of the men. All were convicted of the murder of Sergeant Brett. One of the men, Thomas Maguire, was a serving soldier who had been in the Royal Marines for ten years. He had been on leave and found himself quite by accident in the vicinity of the escape. He was subsequently pardoned and freed to rejoin his regiment. Another man, O'Meagher Condon, had served in the American army. His sentence was commuted to penal servitude, the government being unwilling to provoke an international incident by executing an American citizen on what was generally agreed to be the flimsiest of evidence. The other three, William Philip Allen, Michael Larkin and Michael O'Brien, were to hang. This may seem excessively harsh, but the fact remains that they were all present and participated in the attack on the prison van. When a body of men take part in this way, in a joint enterprise where somebody dies, then all those who have taken part are regarded in law as equally guilty, regardless of who fired the shot, struck the blow or wielded the knife.

The three men who were to hang all made remarkable statements from the dock before sentence was passed upon them. William Allen said:

No man in this court regrets the death of Sergeant Brett more than I do and I positively say, in the presence of the almighty and ever living God, that I am innocent. I don't say this for the sake of mercy: I want no mercy, I'll have no mercy. I will die proudly and triumphantly in defence of republican principles and the liberty of an oppressed and enslaved people.

Michael Larkin spoke next from the dock. He too affirmed his innocence of the charge against him, saying:

I have only got a word or two to say concerning Sergeant Brett. As my friend here said, no one could regret this man's death as much as I do. With regard to the charge of pistols and revolvers and using them, I call my God as witness that I neither used pistols, revolvers nor any instrument that day that would deprive the life of a child, let alone a man. Nor did I go there on purpose to take life away. Certainly my Lords, I do not want to deny that I did go to give aid and assistance to those two noble heroes that were confined in that van.

Larkin went on to make a number of telling points. Among these was that the object of the ambush was to free the prisoners, not kill anybody. These were all fair points, although they did not affect the legal position.

Michael O'Brien spoke more passionately than the other two defendants, saying:

I shall commence by saying that any witness who has sworn anything against me has sworn falsely. I have not had a stone in my possession since I was a boy. I had no pistol in my possession on the day that it is alleged that this outrage was committed.

It was almost certainly true that none of the three men who hanged for the murder of Sergeant Brett actually pulled the trigger of the pistol which killed him. Nevertheless, somebody had to answer for this terrible crime and the law is perfectly clear about the matter. If a body of men and women set out upon an act of violence that might result in somebody's injury and the result is a death, then all members of the group are then guilty of murder. Nor is this just a curiosity of Victorian law; the same principle is still in operation to this day. In early 2010, a group of young men and women pursued a teenage schoolboy into Victoria station, where one of them stabbed him to death. Although only one person wielded a knife that day, the police managed to identify and track down more than a dozen young men and women who were in the mob who chased the victim; all were subsequently charged with his murder. This is the legal principle of joint enterprise in action.

The authorities in Manchester were not inclined to risk any rescue attempt of the three condemned men. The prison was guarded not only by 2,500 constables, both regular and special, but also by detachments of troops. The day for the public execution of William Allen, Michael Larkin and Michael O'Brien had been set for 23 November. The hangman was William Calcraft, now 67 years of age and becoming decidedly too old to carry out such duties. He was famous for his reluctance to adopt the 'long drop', which breaks the necks of those being hanged. By dropping a condemned man for 6ft or so, the neck is broken cleanly, causing instantaneous loss of consciousness and rapid death. Calcraft, though, preferred to stick to the old methods of hanging, which he had been using since he was a young man in his twenties. This entailed a short drop of 3ft or so and almost invariably resulted in the executed man choking to death on the end of the rope.

A crowd estimated at between 8,000 and 10,000 people gathered outside Salford Prison on the morning of 22 November. They had come from all over the country and many of them had spent the night there in order to be sure of good places. The authorities were taking no chances at all of the risk of another armed attempt at a rescue. After the freeing of the two men by an armed mob, many volunteer, part-time constables had been sworn in and if the thousands of officers on duty proved ineffective then a detachment of highlanders and a squadron of cavalry were also in position, ready to support the civil power if the need arose.

The three condemned men were lined up together on the scaffold and as the city's clocks struck eight, they fell simultaneously through the trapdoor. William Allen was fortunate, in that his neck was broken and he died almost at once. The other two men, though, were twitching and jerking convulsively on the end of their ropes and Calcraft climbed down beneath the scaffold to finish off the bungled executions. He did this by hanging on Michael Larkin's legs, choking the life from him until he stopped struggling for breath. The Catholic priest who had been present on the scaffold had followed Calcraft down and was so shocked at what he saw that he forbade the hangman from repeating this undignified procedure on Michael O'Brien. Instead, he held the dying man's hand for the next half hour or so, reciting prayers.

Frederick Engels was living in Manchester at the time of the executions. He wrote that the executions had 'Accomplished the final act of separation between England and Ireland. The only thing the Fenians still lacked were martyrs. They have now been provided with them.'

To see where Michael Barrett fits into the situation it is necessary to know a little of his background.

Following the execution of the so-called Manchester Martyrs, the police were still very keen to track down a number of Fenians operating in the north of England. In particular, they wanted badly to speak to 'Captain' O'Sullivan-Burke. The attempt to seize Chester castle and the abortive uprising in Ireland earlier that year had persuaded the government that they faced an unprecedented crisis. In retrospect, this was perhaps an exaggerated fear. When all is said and done, the Irish nationalists in this country did not really represent a threat to the established order. Nevertheless, the hunt continued and in November the police had an amazing piece of luck.

In London, a detective inspector called James Jacob Thomson was strolling along in Bloomsbury one morning, when he bumped into O'Sullivan-Burke in person. He was not alone, but was accompanied by another man whose name turned out to be Casey. Displaying extraordinary courage, considering what Richard O'Sullivan-Burke was supposed to have done, Detective Inspector Thomson at once arrested both men and marched them off to Holborn police station.

Fearful of another rescue attempt of the kind staged in Manchester, the two captured Fenians were quickly transferred to the Clerkenwell House of Detention, which at that time stood a little to the north of Clerkenwell Road. It has since been demolished and a school built on the site, although the underground cells and storage rooms still remain beneath the school playground. It was a grim, seemingly impregnable place. The prison buildings and exercise yards were surrounded by a massive brick wall, 25ft high and over 2ft thick.

Casey and O'Sullivan-Burke proved to have useful friends in London. Every day cooked meals were brought into the prison for them. They were delivered by a 30-year-old Englishwoman called Anne Justice. The authorities made discreet enquiries and discovered that she was living with an Irishman suspected of being a Fenian sympathiser. Their home was frequently visited by Irish expatriates, many of whom were thought to be Fenians.

As autumn turned to winter, rumours that an attempt was soon to be made to 'spring' Casey and O'Sullivan-Burke reached the governor of

Clerkenwell Prison. As is so often the case, the Fenian organisation contained its share of informers and the police were warned quite plainly that an attempt was to be made to free the two captured men from the prison. A watch was set on Anne Justice and her friends, some of whom had rented a room in Woodbridge Street, overlooking the exercise yard of the prison. Extra guards were drafted in and on 12 December the police had a tip-off that an attempt would be made to rescue the two Fenian prisoners while they were in the exercise yard the next day.

The story of what happened in and around Clerkenwell Prison on that Thursday afternoon is so incredible that unless we had the evidence or a good number of reliable witnesses, it would be hard to credit it. Nevertheless, we do have such evidence. The account which follows is based upon that given in the memoirs of Sir Robert Anderson, formerly assistant commissioner at Scotland Yard. It is backed up by the statement of many witnesses, including police and prison officers.

As a result of the warning that there would be an attempt to break into the prison and free O'Sullivan-Burke and Casey, extra armed prison guards had been posted on the rooftop of Clerkenwell Prison. In addition to this, uniformed police were stationed in the surrounding streets with instructions to be very vigilant for anything out of the ordinary which could indicate that a prison break was about to take place. At about 3.30 p.m., a man wheeled a handcart up Corporation Row, the street next to the prison's exercise yard. Balanced precariously on the cart was a large barrel. Behind the high wall, the prisoners, including O'Sullivan-Burke and Casey, were exercising. As the men walked slowly round the exercise yard, the man in charge of the handcart unloaded his barrel and placed it next to the wall. He then threw a white ball over the wall into the exercise yard. This was a pre-arranged signal to Casey and O'Sullivan-Burke, who both then pretended to have stones in their shoes. On the pretext of removing them, they went to a corner of the yard and crouched down. One of the prison guards saw the ball thrown over the wall. It did not occur to him to report this incident; he instead pocketed the ball and took it home for his son.

What happened next was almost beyond belief. The man on the other side of the wall stuck a fuse in the barrel and tried to light it. It began to sputter and the man ran for cover. The fuse went out. He returned and again lit it and dived for safety. It went out again. By this time, the fuse had become so short that the man evidently felt that it would be unsafe to try to light the thing a third time. He simply loaded the barrel back on to the handcart and left.

Almost incredible to relate, the policeman on duty watched this entire proceeding incuriously. It did not even occur to him to speak to the man. Later that day, he reported what he had seen to his sergeant and it became apparent that an attempt to 'spring' the two Fenians had actually been made on 12 December. Vigilance was increased and even more guards posted around the prison. This made subsequent events all the more amazing.

So ineffectual was the behaviour of the police who were supposedly guarding the prison that day that a few days later the Commissioner of Police, Sir Richard Mayne, offered his resignation to the Home Secretary. It was refused.

Friday 13 December 1867 dawned grey and overcast. It was to be an unlucky day for many of those who lived in the shadow of Clerkenwell Prison. Between 3.30 p.m. and 4 p.m., the prisoners were allowed, under the watchful eyes of armed warders, to pace round the exercise yard. Only a stout wall separated them from Corporation Row and Woodbridge Street. However, due to the state of alert that day, the men were allowed to exercise in the morning instead of the afternoon and were then locked up for the rest of the day. It is easy to imagine the frustration that this must have caused to Casey and O'Sullivan-Burke.

At about 3 p.m., a warder noticed Anne Justice talking to a man in Corporation Row, just beyond the prison wall. They seemed to him to be behaving furtively, so he went to fetch another officer, thinking that this might be part of the escape plot about which they had been warned. However, when he returned, Justice and the man had gone. Later that afternoon, another warder saw Anne Justice. This time she was looking out of the window of a house in Woodbridge Street, which overlooked the prison yard. He counted five men in the room with her and they all seemed to be gazing anxiously towards Corporation Row. At 3.45 p.m. a horse and cart stopped in Corporation Row, near the junction with Woodbridge Street. Two men unloaded a barrel, which they placed against the prison wall. One of the men crossed the road to where a group of boys sat smoking and talking. He produced two fireworks, one of which he gave to the boys. Having begged a light, he returned to the barrel, put the lighted firework in it and ran for his life. Almost unbelievably, this once again took place under the gaze of a police officer.

A few seconds later, the barrel exploded with devastating force. The blast was heard all over London, witnesses describing it as sounding like a discharge of artillery or clap of thunder. A 6oft stretch of the prison wall disintegrated and the front of a row of houses collapsed; over fifty people were buried alive in the rubble. Five of those people were killed outright and within a week another seven had died of their injuries. There were over 120 other casualties, ranging from cuts and bruises to torn off arms and legs. The nearest of the police officers on duty, PC Moriarty, sustained no harm, even though he was close to the bomb when it went off. The only injury caused was to his dignity: all his clothes were blown off in the blast. As the smoke cleared, a group of men ran to the prison wall to inspect the damage. Guards at the prison, mistaking them for Fenian attackers about to rescue Casey and Burke, fired warning shots over their heads. In their cells, the two Irishmen called out for somebody to free them from their cells. Other prisoners, who had not been expecting the explosion, were stunned and silent. In retrospect, it was fortunate for the Irish prisoners that they had not been exercising at the time. The explosion, clearly intended only to breach the wall, would have killed them on the spot.

The gunpowder for the bomb that breached the wall of the Clerkenwell House of Detention had been packed into a large beer barrel. Experiments later carried out revealed that a barrel of that size would hold precisely 548lb of fine grain gunpowder. This is a truly awesome amount of explosives, even for a low explosive like gunpowder. It amounts to around a quarter of a ton. The best modern comparison would be with the kind of low explosives used by the IRA in their campaigns during the 1980s and 1990s. A favourite explosive that was used in large bombs was so-called co-op mix, a combination of ammonium nitrate fertiliser and finely ground sugar, triggered by a small amount of commercial high explosive. In 1996, a bomb made of this mixture and weighing a little less than 1,000lb exploded beneath South Quay station in the Docklands area of east London. Buildings over a wide area were badly damaged and over £85 million worth of damage was caused. The Clerkenwell bomb was a little over half the size of this.

Troops were called in to guard the prison and throughout the night the police and fire brigade worked to rescue those buried in the remains of their homes. Anne Justice and two of her companions were arrested at once. On her first night in custody, Justice tried to hang herself. The two men arrested with her, Timothy Desmond, aged 46, and Jeremiah Allen, 36, were identified as having rented the room in Woodbridge Street. All three were charged with murder.

As the sun rose over London the following day, the extent of the destruction could be seen. Every building in Corporation Row was severely damaged and a number had actually been destroyed. The row of stone houses that had been closest to the blast was reduced to rubble. Around 400 other houses were badly damaged. All the windows within a radius of 200 yards or so had been blown out and chimney pots and tiles had been dislodged from roof tops a quarter of a mile from the explosion. Ironically, the only building that had remained unscathed was the prison itself. Apart from a few broken windows and the destruction of a section of its perimeter wall, it had emerged completely undamaged from Britain's first terrorist bombing.

It is impossible to exaggerate the scale of the panic that followed what became known as the Clerkenwell Outrage. The calls made in the aftermath of the attack for emergency powers to deal with the terrorist threat were exceedingly similar to those being made today by those who feel that existing laws are insufficient to cope with the menace posed by the likes of Al-Qaeda. Troops were mobilised and used to guard public buildings and 20,000 special constables were sworn in over the next few weeks. Even liberal newspapers called for new laws which would require all citizens to carry identification at all times in public: shades of the current identity card debate.

The enrolment of thousands of ordinary citizens into a kind of home guard was, of course, also a suggestion made in this country following the 11 September attacks in 2001. Most of the special constables taken on, however, left after a short while. They had been set to guarding museums, arsenals, gasworks and so on, in the expectation that the Clerkenwell bomb was the signal for a co-ordinated series of attacks against London. It was not, of course. It was clear that whoever had caused the explosion had simply no idea of the enormous amount of damage that an entire barrel of gunpowder would be likely to cause. It was just a miscalculation, albeit an exceedingly deadly one.

Benjamin Disraeli, then Chancellor of the Exchequer and soon to become prime minister, was almost hysterical in his reaction to the Clerkenwell explosion. Lord Derby, the prime minister, was out of London. The day after the attack on the prison, Saturday 14 December, Disraeli wrote to him, saying that 'affairs here are very serious'. On the 16th, Disraeli wrote again to Lord Derby. He said:

I will not trouble you with all the schemes, conferences, hopes, and disappointments, of this busy day. The result is that Colonel Fielding, who has just left my room, has undertaken to ascertain, if possible, the relation between the Fenians in England and the revolutionary societies abroad … There is no doubt that there is a system of organised incendiarism afloat, and we credibly hear of men coming from America, who are to take empty houses in various parts of London, and set them on fire, probably simultaneously. Colonel Fielding would have wished to have grappled with these impending calamities.

The Colonel Fielding to whom he refers was an army officer who had been very active in fighting Fenianism in Ireland. The reference to the possible connection with 'revolutionary societies abroad' was a hint that the Clerkenwell Outrage was being viewed less as a one-off tragic miscalculation by a bungling prison breaker and more as being an indication of the existence of an international terrorist conspiracy. Disraeli went on to suggest that centuries of legal safeguards should be abandoned on the spur of the moment, in the chillingly casual remark: 'Many of the miscreants who are to perpetrate these crimes are now here, and are known – and we can't touch them. I think the Habeas Corpus ought to be suspended.'

Nothing could more clearly illustrate the panicked state of the government than some of Disraeli's comments on the events of that December. He was, after all, at the heart of government and would shortly become prime minister. If what we have seen above seems a little alarming, it was nothing compared to what he next proposed; actions which, as he freely admitted, could precipitate war between this country and the United States. Before he went this far, though, he mentioned that a woman known to him had revealed the existence of a plot to assassinate the queen and her government. He wrote:

She now informs me that, on Saturday morning last, a dying Irishman in one of the London hospitals confessed that, early in the session, there was a plot, quite matured, to blow up the Houses of Parliament by gunpowder introduced through the gas-pipes; but it failed through the House being too well watched. They are going, however, to blow up another prison, but which, though pressed, he refrained from declaring. I have sent this information to Hardy, though silent as to the source. Gunpowder through gas-pipes is a new idea, and worth attention …

Although this really does sound pretty far-fetched, only twenty years later a genuine plot to do just this, assassinate the queen and her ministers at Westminster, was only narrowly averted. On 17 December, Disraeli wrote his most serious and dramatic letter yet to the prime minister:

> Affairs appear to be so serious that last night the Cabinet in town (seven strong) agreed to meet and confer, mainly on the critical condition of the Metropolis. Four Secretaries of State (Northcote away), myself, the Lord Chancellor, and Corry. Hardy's bulletins, some received this morning, were of a most anxious and menacing character: but the chief feature was a telegram from Lord Monck, informing the Duke of Bucks that, some eight days past, a Danish brigantine left New York with a band of thirty men sworn to assassinate H.M. and her Ministers. Lord Monck is not an alarmist, and particularly deprecates the expense of Trans-Atlantic telegrams; but in this instance he requests a telegram of receipt. We have no powers to cope with such circumstances as these, and others which are taking place under our nose. The Duke of Bucks has ascertained that on the day named such a vessel did leave New York and, with the prevailing westerly wind, may be expected to arrive in four or five days. Ostensibly chartered for Dieppe, it is to land its passengers in the Bristol Channel. What are we to do? If they land, and are seized, Habeas Corpus will immediately release them. If stopped on the high seas, we may be involved in a war with America.

Disraeli was, quite plainly, perfectly well aware of the dangers of seizing a ship on the high seas in this way, an act which would, under international law, be at best piracy and at worst an act of war against another country. Despite having already calculated that such an action could have the unintended consequence of starting a war with the United States, he went on to say: 'For my part, I should not hesitate advising seizure, and trusting to a Parliamentary indemnity; but it seems that Habeas Corpus is too strong even for such daring, and that we should violate the law without gaining our purpose.'

In other words, although he knew that what he proposed would be against the law and might risk an international incident leading to war, what actually discouraged him was simply that he didn't think it would work. Disraeli shows us with great clarity how a single terrorist incident can lead to politicians and entire governments losing their heads and running around in a panic. It is sobering to think now that, as a result of a harebrained scheme to free a friend from custody, we could have been plunged into war with America.

The government's explanation for the failure of the police to prevent the attack, which had after all taken place literally under their noses, was made in a statement to the House of Commons. The Home Secretary said:

> It appeared that the mode of carrying out the design of which they had received information did not strike those who were set to watch the out-side of the prison … What their attention was apparently directed to was the undermining of the wall; they thought it would probably be blown up from underneath, and had no conception that it would be blown down in the way it really was done.

With such a feeble explanation as this being offered, it is little wonder that the Commissioner of Police for the metropolis felt honour bound to offer his resignation. The police had been warned that an attempt might be made to burrow under the wall of the prison and so they simply ignored some-body planting a barrel containing a quarter of a ton of gunpowder and setting it off with a firework.

Public reaction to the Clerkenwell Outrage was anger at the Irish in general and the Fenians in particular. There had in some quarters been a kind of sneaking admiration for the Irish nationalists as they struggled to free their homeland from what they saw as a colonial oppressor. Any such sympathy evaporated at once. Karl Marx, who was living in London at the time, was furious about the whole episode. He wrote to his friend Engels: 'The London masses, who have shown great sympathy towards Ireland, will be made wild and driven into the arms of a reactionary government. One cannot expect the London proletarians to allow themselves to be blown up in honour of Fenian emissaries.'

Engels agreed. He said: 'The stupid affair in Clerkenwell was obviously the work of a few specialised fanatics; it is the misfortune of all conspiracies that they lead to such stupidities, because "after all something must happen, after all something must be done".'

Another consequence of the attack was that the government set up the first official Secret Service Department, which was established on the direct instructions of the prime minister, Lord Derby. This was to be a joint army and police section and the aim was to gather intelligence and try to anticipate any further attacks by the Fenians. Although this department did

not last long (it was disbanded shortly after Disraeli became prime minister in 1868), it is notable for being the forerunner of both today's Special
Branch and also MI5. One other action taken at about the same time was
to transfer 622 Adams breach-loading .45 revolvers from the army's arsenal
at the Tower of London and distribute them to police stations in the capital.
Meanwhile, investigations into the Clerkenwell explosion were continuing.

It was obvious from the first that Anne Justice had known nothing of the
plan to detonate a bomb. She had clearly guessed that something illegal had
been planned, but her 'friends' had not thought it wise to discuss the matter
in her presence. Finding herself charged with murder, she did all that she
could to assist the police. She told them that a man called Michael Barrett
had arrived from Glasgow a couple of days earlier and that her companions
had seemed somewhat in awe of him. Desmond and Allen, eager to remove
themselves from the shadow of the gallows, confirmed what she said. Keen
to ingratiate themselves further with the authorities, they suggested that the
police start looking for Barrett among the Irish community of Glasgow.

It was not until 3 January 1868 that the police were able to find and
arrest Barrett in the Scottish city. He was staying at the home of one James
O'Neil, who was also promptly arrested for murder. Barrett was a stevedore
and came to the attention of the police because he was caught practising his
marksmanship with a revolver.

At the beginning of the sensational trial, four men and one woman
stood accused in the dock of the Old Bailey, but Michael Barrett alone
remained at the end to hear the Lord Chief Justice sentence him to death.
The first to leave the dock was Anne Justice. The case against her had been
extremely flimsy and had the crime been a less spectacular one she would
probably not have been charged in the first place. In the event, the jury
decided to acquit her without even hearing the defence case. She left the
dock free, but in tears. Next to be acquitted was James O'Neil. He had
been charged solely because he had rented Michael Barrett a room in
Glasgow for a week or two. Lord Chief Justice Cockburn listened to his
defence submissions and directed the jury to deliver a formal verdict of
not guilty.

Timothy Desmond and Jeremiah Allen had struck a deal with the prosecution, who evidently feared that the great show trial of the Fenians was
about to collapse completely. In exchange for a promise of immunity, they
turned Queen's Evidence and testified that the whole affair was Barrett's
doing. They said that until the moment the bomb exploded they had not

the least idea what was intended. Before they left the court, the prosecution had withdrawn the charges against them.

Perhaps the most unsavoury character in court was a man by the name of Patrick Mullany. He was not charged in connection with the Clerkenwell explosion, but was being held on a separate charge of treason felony. He evidently knew all those in the dock and admitted to having sworn an oath to join the Fenians. Finding his neck in jeopardy, he had turned Queen's Evidence and was free in condemning all his erstwhile comrades. Even the counsel for the Crown seemed to find him a slightly odious figure.

Barrett's counsel, Baker Greene, put up a valiant fight in his client's defence, but it was a hopeless case. The Clerkenwell bomb had caused so much outrage that somebody would have to answer for it. Barrett's defence was one of alibi. He had, he claimed, been in Glasgow on the day of the massacre. He produced no fewer than six witnesses who were prepared to swear on oath that he was in Glasgow, getting a pair of boots mended, on the day of the explosion. That the description of the man who had detonated the bomb was of a man over 6ft tall (Barrett was only 5ft 6in) was refuted by two warders from the prison and one of the boys to whom he had spoken in Corporation Row, to say nothing of the landlady of the house in Woodbridge Street. All put him definitely in the vicinity when the bomb had gone off. Evidence was also given that he was an expert in explosives and that the police in Ireland suspected him of belonging to the Irish Republican Brotherhood.

After hearing a very fair and impartial summing up, the jury brought in a verdict of guilty. Upon being asked if he had anything to say before sentence of death was passed, Barrett made a memorable and impressive speech. He said:

> If it is murder to love Ireland more deeply than life, then indeed I am a murderer. If it should please the God of justice to turn to some account, for the benefit of my suffering country, the sacrifice of my poor, worthless life, I could by the grace of God ascend the scaffold with firmness, strengthened by the consoling reflection that the stain of murder did not rest upon me.

He spoke calmly, without notes, and even Lord Chief Justice Cockburn seemed impressed. A number of women in the public gallery were reduced to tears and by the end of his speech, one or two had actually fainted. Sentence of death was then pronounced and Barrett was removed to the condemned cell of Newgate Prison, which at that time stood close to the site of the modern-day Old Bailey.

Before his execution a special commission was appointed to look into his claim that he had been in Glasgow at the time of the explosion. It was, as *The Times* remarked, tantamount to a second trial. It came to nothing. The witnesses who had claimed to have seen Barrett in Glasgow on the day of the outrage were all Irish republicans and therefore hardly unbiased. The commission visited Glasgow and Clerkenwell, re-examining all the evidence. They concluded that there had been no miscarriage of justice and that the law should take its course.

On the last day of his life, Barrett rose at six o'clock. A Catholic priest stayed with him until the end. Shortly before eight, William Calcraft, the hangman, came to Barrett's cell to pinion him. Calcraft was by this time a doddery old man who had been public executioner for almost forty years. Outside the cell, four warders waited. They escorted the condemned man to the press room, where they were joined by the sheriff and under sheriffs. The prison bell tolled and Calcraft led the solemn procession through a small side door that took them out to the scaffold. As they emerged into the pale, early morning sun there were cries among the crowd of 'Hats off'. This was not a sign of respect, but simply a desire to have a better view. In the windows overlooking the black painted gallows, well-dressed men and fashionable women trained binoculars and opera glasses on the scene below them.

Calcraft went up the steps first and began preparing the rope. He was followed by the priest and then Barrett, escorted by two warders. As Barrett stepped into view beneath the gallows, cheers from the crowd were immediately drowned by hisses and catcalls. They slowly died away until there was utter silence. Barrett stood, his face pinched and pale, as Calcraft pulled a white hood over his head and placed the rope around his neck. Turning to the hangman, Barrett asked him to loosen the rope a little, which was done. Then Calcraft pulled the lever. As the condemned man fell through the trapdoor, the crowd gave an almighty roar, part scream and part groan. A large number of people remained for another hour to watch Calcraft take down the body. There were jeers and cries of 'Come on body snatcher, take away the man you killed!'

Although he has now been almost completely forgotten, Michael Barrett did achieve immortality of a sort. After his execution, his name became synonymous with 'Irishman'. Irish men found themselves being referred to disparagingly as 'Mick Barretts'. Over the course of time, this became abbreviated to 'Micks', a derogatory expression which is still employed today for the Irish.

The Clerkenwell explosion was not, after all, the opening shot in a great terrorist campaign against the capital, despite the fears of politicians like Disraeli and Lord Derby. It was a one-off, a freak event which was never intended to kill anybody or indeed cause any great damage to any property apart from the prison. That is not how it appeared at the time, though. To many people, even in the government, it seemed that the nation was under threat from within. Disraeli's fantastic account of gunpowder being intro-duced into the Houses of Parliament via the gas pipes has all the hallmarks of the sort of anticipated Al–Qaeda assault which justifies the imposition of identity cards and the passing of laws which will overturn the principle of habeas corpus and allow for imprisonment without trial. The Clerkenwell Outrage served as a warning of what to expect in the next few years.

4

THE FIRST MODERN
TERRORIST CAMPAIGN

Terrorism as we understand it today, that is to say random attacks which jeopardise the lives and property of ordinary people, began in England. The Clerkenwell explosion was, of course, not intended to kill and maim innocent victims nor was it designed to destroy their homes, although the perpetrators were certainly indifferent to the consequences of exploding a large barrel of gunpowder in a crowded street of the largest city on Earth. Terrorism is something else entirely. The aim of terrorist attacks is to cause terror in the population for political ends. It is true that organisations such as *Narodnaya Volya* in Tsarist Russia used bombs in their struggle against the autocracy, but these were part of a strategy of targeted assassinations against officials of the state rather than passers-by. It is also true that some chance individuals died in this way, caught as it were in the crossfire of the battle between the revolutionaries and the forces of the Tsarist state. Such deaths were, however, accidental, an unfortunate by-product. In fact, the bomb throwers of the *Narodnaya Volya* would delay an assassination if there seemed to be a chance that passers-by might be killed or injured. Today's terrorists, on the other hand, wish to create terror by killing passengers on trains and aeroplanes for no other reason than to draw attention to their cause. It is this type of terrorism which has its roots in Victorian London.

After 1867, there was a lull of fifteen years or so; long enough for many people to persuade themselves that the threat from Irish extremism had ended. In fact the opposite was true. Having failed in their efforts to spark a popular uprising in Ireland itself, the Fenian movement had decided upon what seemed to them a far better strategy: holding British cities to

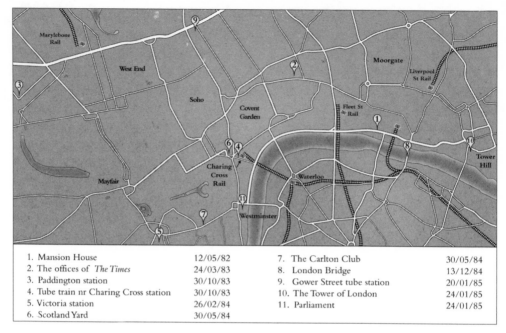

1. Mansion House	12/05/82	7. The Carlton Club	30/05/84
2. The offices of *The Times*	24/03/83	8. London Bridge	13/12/84
3. Paddington station	30/10/83	9. Gower Street tube station	20/01/85
4. Tube train nr Charing Cross station	30/10/83	10. The Tower of London	24/01/85
5. Victoria station	26/02/84	11. Parliament	24/01/85
6. Scotland Yard	30/05/84		

Fenian bombings.

ransom in order to force the hand of the government in London. It was an early realisation of something which the Provisional IRA rediscovered in the 1970s – that one bomb exploding in an English city is worth ten such attacks in Belfast or Londonderry.

The mastermind behind the bombing campaign of the 1880s was a man called Jeremiah O'Donovan Rossa, who led a breakaway group of Fenians who had split from the Irish Republican Brotherhood to form their own organisation, called Clan na Gael. He had been tried for high treason in 1865 and sentenced to life imprisonment for his part in planning a rising in Ireland. While in prison he was elected to Parliament for the constituency of Tipperary, although being a convicted felon he was unable to take his seat in the Commons. He was released from prison in 1870 as part of an amnesty and went into voluntary exile in the United States, where he set about organising groups of men who became known as Rossa's Skirmishers. It was these men who travelled to England to plant bombs.

The first bomb of the new campaign was planted near Salford barracks in Manchester on 14 January 1881. It exploded with devastating effect, injuring four civilians who happened to be nearby at the time. One of them, a

7-year-old boy, died from his injuries two days later. The next attack took place in London.

Wednesday 16 March 1881 was a cold and foggy day in London. The Mansion House, official residence of the Lord Mayor of London, was in darkness. A grand banquet had originally been planned for that night, but it had been cancelled out of respect, following the assassination of Tsar Alexander II by the *Narodnaya Volya* movement in Russia. At about 11.30 p.m., a small group of men carried a large wooden box into an alleyway behind the Mansion House. This crate contained 15lb of explosives and it was to deliver the opening shot in what became known as the Dynamite War. Having lit the fuse sticking out of this box, the men ran swiftly off. By an amazing stroke of luck, Constable Samuel Cowell strolled past just as the fuse had almost reached the charge. There was less than an inch to go, but PC Cowell did not hesitate. He reached out and extinguished the smouldering fuse casually, as though he was snuffing out a candle. Then he simply picked up the box of explosives, placed it under his arm like a parcel and took it to the police station at Bow Lane. It was an anti-climactic ending to what was originally planned as an act of mass murder.

It was the invention of dynamite in 1867 that made terrorism of the sort carried out in the 1880s practical. We saw in an earlier chapter the difficulties involved with using nitroglycerine for bombs. Gunpowder is safer to use and easier to make, but it is a bulky and not particularly powerful explosive. Dynamite was completely safe, easy to use and provided a very convenient way of building bombs. It was the perfect weapon for the terrorist, called by some 'the poor man's artillery'. As a newspaper of the time observed: 'A single wayfarer, with dynamite in his pocket throws the cities of England into greater terror than would a hundred thousand men landing at Dover.'

Although the offices of Scotland Yard were attacked by this means a few years later, the great majority of the bombs planted during this particularly vicious campaign were aimed solely at ordinary Londoners going about their day-to-day affairs. Many of the places targeted were familiar landmarks. This campaign also saw the first bomb explosions on the capital's tube trains. Most of those conducting the attacks were Irish Americans. After the defused bomb at the Mansion House, there was a pause of two months before the planting of the next bomb. It is clear that the Mansion House bomb was originally intended to be what the IRA now call a 'spectacular', which would have struck at a glittering crowd of the great and good who should by rights have been feasting at the Mansion House on 16 March. It must have been a great disappointment to those who planned this when they realised that the banquet had been cancelled; an even greater disappointment when PC Cowell strolled past at the critical moment and prevented the device from exploding at all.

The next explosion was in the north of England, when the police headquarters in Liverpool was damaged. A short while later, another device exploded outside Liverpool town hall. In June, a police barracks in Edinburgh was damaged by an explosion. None of these incidents attracted much attention and the Fenians decided that only bombs in the capital itself were likely to have any real effect upon public opinion. A year after the Liverpool bombs on 12 May 1882, another attempt was made to blow up the Mansion House in London. This time the bomb did not explode properly, causing no damage at all to the building. A year later, the bombers returned to London, only this time they were far more efficient.

It was becoming quite clear that ordinary police methods were not sufficient to deal with this new threat to the security of the country. Painstaking police work could certainly track down the terrorists after they had planted their bombs and ensure that they were brought to justice, and there had been some successes in fighting back against the Fenians. On 16 June, for instance, a Fenian arms dump was raided in Clerkenwell, near to the site of the Clerkenwell Outrage fifteen years previously. It contained 400 rifles, 60 pistols and 80,000 bullets. What was needed, though, was a more proactive approach; hunting the bombers down before they were able to strike. Lord Derby's short-lived Secret Service Department had been disbanded in May 1868, once it had become clear that there was no real danger from the Irish Republican Brotherhood. The Clerkenwell explosion had, of course, been a one off, an accident rather than a deliberate act of terror. The bombs being placed during this new Fenian activity were quite different. So on 17 March 1883, Assistant Commissioner Howard Vincent selected twelve men, four of them from the CID, to form a new Special Irish Branch. Their role would essentially be counter-intelligence, finding out what the terrorists were planning and frustrating their actions before they had a chance to cause any harm. This unit was supposedly a strictly short-term measure to respond to an emergency and it was always intended to disband this department as soon as the bombings came to an end. However, nothing lasts like the temporary and after dropping the word 'Irish' from its name, the Special Branch is still going strong well over a hundred years later.

1 Aftermath of the explosion at the Tower of London, which took place on the same day as the two bombs at Parliament. (*The Graphic*, 31 January 1885)

2 The ultimate nightmare: Big Ben and St Paul's Cathedral destroyed by terrorist strikes. Illustrations from a novel published in 1892.

3 The site of the 1894 bomb attack on Greenwich Observatory.

4 The site of the Aldersgate station tube bombing of 1897. The station is now called Barbican.

5 The aftermath of the April 1897 tube bombing. The carriage torn apart by the explosion.

6 A bizarre souvenir of the 1897 tube bombing: an inkwell made from fragments of the carriage destroyed by the explosion.

7 Armed police at the Battle of Stepney in 1911. Their old shotguns could not hope to compete with the modern, semi-automatic weapons of the terrorists.

8 The Scots Guards exchanging shots with the terrorists during the Battle of Stepney.

9 Cutler Street, the site of the 1910 Houndsditch police murders, today. Although it is now a through road, at the time of the shootings a row of houses made this street a cul-de-sac.

10 A recently unveiled memorial to the three dead police officers. It is placed at the scene of the murders in Cutler Street.

11 The Manchester Martyrs, three men hanged for the murder of a police officer.

IN MEMORY OF
WILLIAM FREDERICK TYLER
POLICE CONSTABLE 403 OF 'N' DIVISION
METROPOLITAN POLICE SERVICE

FALLEN WHILE BRAVELY SERVING THE COMMUNITY
ON THE 23rd JANUARY 1909

ERECTED BY THE OFFICERS OF HARINGEY BOROUGH POLICE
AND THE COMMUNITY ON THE CENTENARY OF
'THE TOTTENHAM OUTRAGE'

Above: 12 A commemorative plaque on the side of Tottenham police station to PC Tyler, shot dead in 1909 during the Tottenham Outrage.

13 PC Tyler's grave in Abney Park cemetery in Stoke Newington. The sculpted helmet and police cape even bear Tyler's police number.

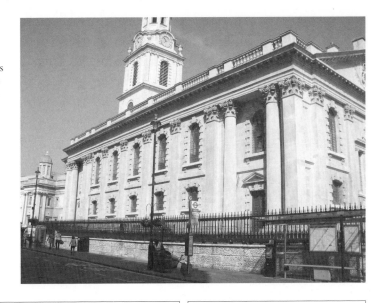

14 The south side of St Martin-in-the-Fields church today. The windows were blown out by a bomb planted by suffragettes.

BOMB EXPLODED IN LONDON CHURCH

Suffragettes Attempt to Wreck St. Martin's-in-the-Fields at Every Service.

By Marconi Transatlantic Wireless Telegraph to The New York Times. •

MILITANTS BLOW UP CORONATION CHAIR

Bomb in Westminster Abbey Wrecks Historic Relic and Damages Altar Screen.

NEW PLAN TO END OUTRAGES

Government to Prosecute Civilly and Criminally Subscribers to Suffragette War Chest.

Special Cable to THE NEW YORK TIMES.

Above: 15 Newspaper headlines about the suffragette bombings of churches in 1914.

16 The Bank of England, site of an attempted bombing by the suffragettes in 1913.

17 The climax of the Fenian dynamite campaign. Bomb damage at Parliament following the attack on Saturday 24 January 1885. (*The Graphic*, 31 January 1885)

The newly formed Special Branch had its first success in October, when they were able to identify one of the chief bomb makers, a man called Thomas Gallagher. He was arrested in Liverpool along with five other men. During the raid, an almost unbelievable 500lb of explosives was also seized.

On 24 March 1883, there was an explosion at the offices of *The Times* newspaper. Meanwhile, in the Midlands, the police had had a success. One group of terrorists had been manufacturing its own explosives by bulk buying sulphuric acid and other ingredients. This had not unnaturally drawn attention to them and resulted in the discovery of a bomb factory which contained over 400lb of high explosive. Such was the serious nature of this new form of terrorism that the decision was made to charge the men found in possession of the explosives with treason felony. In other words, they were accused of waging war against the state. Thomas Gallagher and three other men were all sentenced to life imprisonment after a trial before the Lord Chief Justice.

British governments have traditionally responded to crises of this sort with hasty and ill-thought out legislation rushed through in a hurry. The Dynamite War provoked just such a piece of legislation. The Explosive Substances Act was hastily passed a few days after Gallagher's trial in 1883. The act provided a minimum sentence of two years' imprisonment for the possession of explosive substances. Controversially, it reversed the burden of proof in such cases. Anybody found in possession of explosives was assumed to have them unlawfully; the onus was on the defendant to show that he did not have the explosives with criminal intent. To the dismay of some MPs, this bill was rushed through both Houses of Parliament in a matter of hours, leaving little time for debate.

There was then another lull in the campaign. Then in the autumn, the attacks resumed with even greater ferocity. At five past eight in the evening of 30 October 1883, a bomb exploded in a tunnel of the Metropolitan Line, near Paddington station. A number of passengers were injured, some seriously, by flying glass. A few minutes later, another explosion took place between Charing Cross and Westminster stations. This time there were fifty casualties, although thankfully nobody was killed. This was the first time that the London Underground had been targeted by terrorists. Shortly after these explosions, time bombs were placed in left-luggage lockers at mainline railway stations.

Although most of the Fenian activity was in London, there were a few attacks in other parts of Britain. In Glasgow in 1883, for instance, there were dynamite explosions at a railway station, gasworks and bridges.

In February 1884, a bomb exploded in the left-luggage office at Victoria station. There were no injuries, though, and three other devices left at railways stations were discovered and defused.

Early in the summer of 1884, Rossa's Skirmishers scored an astonishing propaganda victory over the newly formed Special Irish Branch. Superintendent Adolphus Williamson was the head of the Special Irish Branch and the men of Clan na Gael knew it. They sent an anonymous letter to the police, threatening to blow Superintendent Williamson 'off his stool' on 30 May 1884. Security was tightened and the men at Scotland Yard were quite convinced that nobody could possibly get close enough to do any harm. A constable was posted outside Scotland Yard, with instructions to keep an eye out for anything at all suspicious. On the night of 30 May, however, a large bomb exploded in a cast-iron urinal just yards from Scotland Yard. Superintendent Williamson's office was wrecked and many of his confidential files on Irish activists were destroyed. It was a fantastic coup for the Fenians. On the same night, a bomb exploded outside the Carlton Club and an enormous device containing sixteen sticks of dynamite was found at the foot of Nelson's Column. Fortunately, this was discovered before it exploded and it proved possible to defuse it safely.

The attack on Scotland Yard was a tremendous blow to the prestige of the police. It also became the archetype for similar terrorist actions right up to the present day. One of the most notable features of this particular incident is the complete and utter disregard for the lives of others. The dynamite was timed to explode at 9 p.m. It is true that Scotland Yard itself was pretty deserted at that time of the evening, but the cast-iron men's urinal in which it was concealed was only a few yards from a busy pubic house, the Rising Sun. There were about twenty casualties in the pub and it is something of a miracle that nobody was killed. The most seriously injured was the policeman on guard duty outside Scotland Yard. In the pub, a number of customers were cut by flying glass and a barmaid almost bled to death from a severed artery. It is little short of a miracle that nobody had been killed.

The most embarrassing aspect of the Scotland Yard attack was that the secret files which the Special Branch had been painstakingly compiling were destroyed by the explosion. Especially galling was the fact that the files on the Irish Republican Brotherhood were lost in the explosion.

Meanwhile, the newly formed Special Irish Branch was having quiet success in deterring the bombers before they struck, rather than tracking them down after the event. They faced many of the same problems which anti-terrorist agencies in Britain are struggling with today. Chief among these was the continuing problem of the traditional 'open borders' policy which this country had operated from time immemorial. Anybody at all was free to enter the country and live here as long as they pleased. It would be another twenty years before the first British immigration act, the 1905 Aliens Act, changed all this.

In 1884, though, our borders were still very much 'porous', to use the modern expression. Fenian subversives were free to travel to and from America and the Continent without any records being kept or any attempt being made to prevent them from entering the country. William Melville, an Irish-born member of the Special Irish Branch, helped to set up a system of keeping watch upon ports for any potential troublemakers. When, a few years ago, British police and border officials were posted to Calais in order to supervise screening for those hoping to enter this country from France, it was portrayed as a radically new way of handling immigration and terrorism. It was nothing of the sort. In 1884, William Melville was posted to the French port of La Havre for exactly the same purpose. He spent four years there, arranging that the documents of all those taking ships to England should be examined.

Londoners have become quite stoical about the various security precautions which seem to have become a permanent way of life in the capital. Bag searches, travel delayed by security checks; we regard such things as a modern inconvenience. The Victorians too ended up taking these things in their stride. Railway journeys took longer because of security checks and guards scrutinised visitors to well-known public attractions. Other, less obtrusive measures were also adopted. Security grills designed to prevent bombs from being placed in actual contact with the fabric of bridges were one such precaution. Some thought them a waste of time, but they proved their value on 13 December 1884.

At about 6 p.m. three men in a rowing boat moored under London Bridge and while two of them tried to steady the craft, which was bobbing about in the water, the third attempted to attach a large device containing nitroglycerine to one of the newly installed security grills on the underside of the bridge. Even under ideal conditions, nitroglycerine can be tricky stuff to handle, and the conditions in the tiny rowing boat on a windy winter's night in the middle of the Thames were far from ideal.

The explosion that occurred was described by passers-by on the bridge as sounding like a clap of thunder. The three men in the dinghy, William Francis Lomasney, his brother-in-law Peter Malon and John Fleming were killed instantly. At first, the police were unsure whether they were in fact dead and offered a reward of £5,000 for information leading to their capture. However, over the next few weeks, bits of the three men turned up on the Thames foreshore.

The following year, the terrorists struck again at the Tube. On 20 January there was an explosion on the Metropolitan Line near Gower Street station, now renamed Euston Square. It appeared that one of the passengers had thrown a bomb on to the track from a train. The police, already at a high state of alert, sealed off Gower Street station before the train arrived. All the passengers were questioned and the police took special note of an Irishman, about whom they had suspicions. Unfortunately, in the general chaos on the platform, with hysterical passengers and the removal of several people injured by the explosion, this man managed to slip away. The name he gave was Cunningham and his narrow escape from the scene of the Gower Street bombing does not seem to have alarmed him unduly.

Four days later, the Fenians used a tactic which has been used to deadly effect in more recent terrorist campaigns: the so-called 'come-on' bomb. The way that this method works is by exploding a relatively small device which then panics a crowd into running towards a larger and more deadly bomb. Saturdays were the only days that Victorian women were allowed into the palace of Westminster. They were therefore very popular days out for families. On 24 January 1884, the Houses of Parliament were crowded with visitors. As a group of women were walking down the steps leading into St Stephen's crypt, one of them happened to glance down and see a smouldering package. She screamed a warning and other visitors fled. At that moment, the device went off. It threw a number of people to the ground and caused some superficial damage to an ornamental iron gate.

As the crowds fled from this first bomb, a second exploded, actually in the chamber of the Commons. This caused a great deal of damage, blowing out all the windows and shattering the benches. It created absolute panic and a number of women were injured in the rush to escape. At about the same time that these two bombs exploded, a device was detonated in the Tower of London, the symbol of security and strength in the capital. This bomb went off in the White Tower itself and shattered almost every window on one floor, showering sightseers with broken glass. The gates to the Tower of London were closed and nobody allowed out until they had been properly identified. It was hoped that the person who planted the bomb would not have had time to escape.

At both the Tower of London and Houses of Parliament, angry crowds gathered. They were incensed at the sight of children being brought out with cuts and bruises, in some cases covered with blood. There were cries of 'Lynch the villains' and 'Roast the fiends'. There can be no doubt at all that there was very definitely a sense of hostility towards the Irish inhabitants of London in general and not just the Fenian bombers themselves.

The prompt action of the beefeaters in closing the gates to the Tower ensured that the bomber was caught. His real name was James George Gilbert and he was 22 years old. He was the same man who had been questioned at Gower Street station. His arrest was really due as much to luck on the part of the police as anything else. They were paying special attention to any Irish sightseers whom they found among those visiting the Tower of London that day and Gilbert made matters worse for himself by initially giving a false address. As ill luck would have it for the bomber, the part of London where he claimed to be living was well known to the policeman questioning him and it did not take very long to see that there was something out of the ordinary about young Gilbert.

On searching him, the police found evidence of his real address and they sent a squad round to search the premises. Gilbert's room contained a wealth of incriminating material, including detonators that could only be used for setting off a charge of dynamite. With the information found at James Gilbert's lodgings, the Fenian cell began to unravel fast. An accomplice called Henry Burton was arrested and the trail led officers of the Special Irish Branch to a house in Harrow Road, west London. There they uncovered an enormous cache of explosives, an astonishing 50lb of dynamite, in fact, over half a hundredweight.

With the arrests of James Gilbert and Henry Burton, the bombing campaign on the British mainland was almost brought to an end. The charges on which the two men were arraigned at the Old Bailey are curious. During some of the recent IRA and Al-Qaeda activity in this country, the idea has been mooted that it might be possible to charge those carrying out attacks against Britain with treason, rather than offences against the Explosive Substances Act. The reasoning behind this is that those planting explosive devices here are, in effect, levying war against the sovereign, which is one of the elements of treason.

When the police were drawing up charges against Gilbert and Burton, a law officer for the Crown told them that because the Tower of London was officially a royal palace, the attack upon it could indeed be classed as high treason. In the end, compromise was reached and the actual charge was Treason Felony, the same used against Thomas Gallagher. The indictment charged that Gilbert and Burt were:

> Indicted under the Treason Felony Act of 1848 for feloniously conspiring with other persons whose names are unknown to depose the Queen from her Royal name and style of Queen of Great Britain and Ireland. Also for conspiring to levy war against the Queen with intent by force and constraint to compel her to change her measures and to intimidate and overawe the Houses of Parliament.

The trial took place at the Old Bailey on 20 April 1885. By making the charge one of Treason Felony, rather than detailing specific incidents for which the two men were responsible, the prosecution was able to pile on as much evidence as they felt inclined. The bomb at Victoria station was mentioned, as were the attacks on the Houses of Parliament, Tower of London and, of course, Gower Street station. The case for the prosecution was comprehensive and watertight, implicating both Gilbert and Burton in a series of bombs. It was lucky for the men that they had been charged under the Treason Felony Act rather than with high treason, which of course carried a mandatory death sentence. After the verdict of guilty was brought in, both were sentenced to life imprisonment.

It appeared to most people, as 1885 and then 1886 passed, that the Fenian dynamiters were a spent force. There was, however, one last episode, a deadly conspiracy which had it been successful would have changed the course of world history. It became known as the Jubilee Plot.

The Jubilee Plot

The date 20 June 1887 was to be one of rejoicing throughout the whole of the British Empire. Queen Victoria would have been on the throne for fifty years and London was to be the scene of unprecedented celebrations. The event would culminate with a service of thanksgiving in Westminster Abbey, attended by the queen, the royal family and the entire Cabinet. In other words, the head of state and her government would all be assembled together in one place at the same time. We are all of us familiar with the plot to blow up the monarch and his government which so nearly succeeded on

5 November 1605. Indeed, we still celebrate King James' deliverance from this audacious enterprise by burning the chief conspirator in the affair in effigy on the anniversary of the plot's failure. Few know that a precisely similar plan was hatched a little over 250 years later and that preparations were well advanced for the destruction in a massive terrorist attack of the whole British Government and royal family, including the queen.

After the petering out of the Fenian dynamite campaign of the 1880s, there was a gap of two years. Many hoped that the danger was now at an end and that the Irish terrorists based in the USA had at last realised that British Government policy towards Ireland was not to be swayed by a few bombs exploding on the streets of the capital. In fact, the Fenians who had masterminded the bombing campaign in London had also reached this conclusion. There were no more random bomb outrages after 1885. Instead, the leadership in America decided to try another tactic, a 'blow to the centre' as it was called by the Russian terrorist groups operating at this time. An attempt would be made to mount what we would today describe as a 'spectacular': a terrorist attack which the government would be unable to ignore, one which would bring the cause of Irish independence firmly to the centre of the stage not just in this country, but throughout the entire world.

There is in military circles a term for an attack of this kind; it is known as a 'decapitation strike'. The head of the British body politic would, in a fraction of a second, be removed. This shockingly unexpected action would leave the country leaderless and be the signal for rebels in Ireland to rise up against their oppressors.

We know the names of three of the men who were involved in this astonishing plan. Thomas Callan was one of them. He was a 46-year-old Irishman who had been living in the United States for some years. Another was 30-year-old Michael Harkins. The other was 'General' Francis Millen, a leading figure in the Irish-American revolutionary movement. It was he who arranged for Callan and Harkins to be supplied with a huge quantity of dynamite and sufficient funds to enable them to book a passage to Liverpool. On 11 June 1887, the two bombers sailed from New York with enough explosives to kill hundreds of people and probably destroy Westminster Abbey in the process.

The 90lb of dynamite which Thomas Callan and Michael Harkins carried in their luggage when they embarked on the sea crossing to Liverpool is a truly awe-inspiring amount of high explosives. To give some idea of the amount of damage which might be wrought by this quantity of commercial explosives it is instructive to look at a few of the IRA bombings that took place in this country in the 1970s and 1980s. In 1974, two bombs exploded in public houses in Guildford that were frequented by service men and women. In addition to the casualties, these bombs caused major structural damage to the buildings in which they exploded. Each bomb contained an estimated 5lb of explosive. On the early morning of 12 October 1984, an IRA bomb exploded in the Grand Hotel on the seafront at Brighton. The intention was to kill the prime minister, Margaret Thatcher, and also as many of her Cabinet as possible. In the event, only five people died in the attack, but the front of the hotel was brought down by the force of the explosion. This bomb contained only about 20lb of gelignite, less than a quarter of the amount that Callan and Harkins planned to detonate in Westminster Abbey.

It is probably fair to say that had 90lb of commercial explosive been detonated in Westminster Abbey, then the course of world history would have been dramatically changed. Various other world leaders would have been present at the service and they too would most likely have been killed by an explosion of this size. This is to say nothing of the very real possibility that the abbey itself might have collapsed under the pressure of such an explosion taking place within a confined space. Buildings are constructed to withstand substantial external force in the form of wind. None are built to tolerate a pressure wave from within. This would particularly be the case with a building like Westminster Abbey, which dates back to the Middle Ages.

In the event, the whole project miscarried almost before it had begun. The steamship *City of Chester*, upon which the terrorists were travelling, was delayed and did not reach Liverpool until 21 June, the day after the grand jubilee celebrations had taken place. This may have averted the immediate danger, but it still left two armed and desperate terrorists on the loose in Britain with an enormous cache of high explosives. The two men made for London and soon found lodgings in the capital. Callan first stayed at a house in south London and then two months later moved to 24 Baxter Road, Islington, where a Mrs Bright and her daughter rented him a room. Harkins was lodging nearby at 9 Alfred Street.

Three more characters enter the plot at this point. One was Joseph Cohen, who was allegedly the paymaster of the terrorist cell to which Callan and Harkins belonged. Another was 'General' Millen, who had also moved to

London. What nobody seemed to realise was that Millen, high in the councils of the Fenian movement for many years, was in fact a double agent working for the British Government. We shall see later that it has been suggested in recent years that he was himself the architect of the entire plan to bomb the abbey and, according to some sources, he was acting under the direct instructions of the prime minister, Lord Salisbury. The third man was Joseph Moroney, otherwise known as Joseph Melville. He was seen a number of times in the company of Callan and Harkins, even visiting Parliament with them.

The year 1887 was very important for Irish politics. The previous year, Gladstone had formed his third administration with the stated aim of 'pacifying Ireland'. He was supported in his aim by the charismatic figure of Charles Parnell, an Irish MP. Some type of home rule for Ireland looked as though it might be a distinct possibility in the coming years and there were those who sought to sabotage this. Linking Irish MPs with a terrorist plot to murder the queen would have been the perfect way to achieve this end.

On 4 August, Harkins and Melville were seen at the House of Commons. Police Inspector William Horsely was present when the two men came to Parliament to see an Irish nationalist MP called Joseph Nolan. They came back the following day and were seen to be deep in discussion with him. Inspector Horsely had also seen Thomas Callan in various parts of the House, including St Stephen's Hall. This does not seem as though they were reconnoitring the place with a view to blowing it up; more that they were planning something with an Irish MP. Joseph Nolan later denied knowing who Harkins and Melville were, claiming that he could not remember them at all.

It seems highly likely in view of subsequent events that the police were watching Callan, Melville/Moroney and Harkins for the whole of this time. Questions were later raised as to why, if this was so, no attempt was made to arrest them. Perhaps the police were playing a long game, as they do today when keeping terrorist suspects under observation. They may well have been waiting to see who else these men would lead them to. If so, this was a dangerous strategy, bearing in mind that the players in this particular conspiracy had at their disposal the best part of a hundredweight of high explosives.

For the next month, Harkins and Callan lived quietly in Islington. On the night of 10 September, Thomas Callan had a visitor. We cannot be sure, but it seems likely that his visitor was Michael Harkins. At any rate, his landlady, Mrs Bright, said that a man came to see her lodger and that the two men carried a box into his room. She heard them carrying the trunk into Callan's room and said that it sounded as though they were carrying something very heavy. The following day, she and her daughter went into Callan's room while he was out. Ostensibly, they were going to tidy up, but it is hard to escape the conclusion that they were being nosy and wished to see what this heavy trunk was that their lodger had brought home. They found that the box was so heavy that they were quite unable to move it. It was locked.

We can only guess what Callan, Harkins, Melville and Cohen were up to during this time. Nor can we know at this late stage what the connection was between them and the MP Joseph Nolan. Were they trying to find another target for a 'spectacular' bomb attack? We shall never know.

On 19 October, the police struck. They arrived at Harkins' lodgings in Alfred Street with a warrant to search the premises. A quantity of money was found as well as a loaded revolver. They asked him to give some account of himself and he mentioned that he had a friend living in Lambeth Road on the other side of London. When the police went to the address given, they were told that the man whom Harkins had suggested that they see was living in the back room. This was not quite correct. The man, Joseph Cohen, was in the back room all right, but he was not living. He had died from tuberculosis and his corpse was lying in the bed. The police found money and a loaded pistol in his room as well.

Now for whatever reason, either because they did not know where he was living or because they wished to see to whom he might lead them, the police made no effort to bring in Thomas Callan. His position was now an unenviable one. The man who supplied him with money was dead and his comrade had been arrested. Within a few days, he had decided that the best thing he could do was to dispose of the vast quantity of dynamite which he was keeping in a trunk under his bed. There was so much of it, though, that he didn't know what to do with it and so started to break open the cartridges, crumble it up and throw some down the lavatory. It is hard to believe that anybody could behave in such a mad fashion and yet the records of the trial set out his actions vividly.

On 27 October, his landlady, Mrs Bright, discovered that the outside lavatory was completely blocked with what she thought was crumbled up mortar or dried cement. She could not clear it all out and so engaged a workman to do so. He managed to clear the lavatory, piling about 5lb of what he too took to be old cement or lime in the dustbin. Charles Johns, who lived next door with his elderly mother, found some of the 'mortar' in the dustbin a week later. It was damp and for some inexplicable reason, he later said it would be useful for the pigeons he kept, and decided to dry the stuff in his mother's oven.

On the afternoon of 8 November, old Mrs Johns' oven exploded with considerable force. Fortunately, nobody was hurt. It transpired that Thomas Callan had tried to dispose of his dynamite by flushing it away down the lavatory and it was some of this which Charles Johns had dried in the oven. Ten days later, Callan went to the Bank of England to change some banknotes. Without the help of Joseph Cohen, he seemed not to be well acquainted with the correct method for endorsing notes and obtaining change for them. He appeared to have a number of different names and addresses and so the cashier sent for the police. It was while searching his room that the police uncovered his cache of dynamite and recognised it for what it was.

Callan and Harkins were both charged with conspiring to cause an explosion likely to endanger life and cause serious damage to property. No mention was made in court of the plot to blow up Westminster Abbey. At the conclusion of the trial, verdicts of guilty were brought in and both men were sent to prison for fifteen years.

Melville and Francis Millen escaped back to America. In recent years, the idea has been mooted that the entire plot was really a cunning manoeuvre by Lord Salisbury, the prime minister. He certainly initialled some of the documents connected with the activities of Francis Millen. The theory is that a plan was hatched to put a stop to Charles Stewart Parnell, the brilliant Irish MP who was working towards independence or home rule for Ireland. Parnell was vulnerable on several fronts. For one thing, he lived with a married woman who bore him two children. In Victorian times this was such a shocking state of affairs that when it became common knowledge in the 1890s, this scandal alone was enough to end Parnell's political aspirations.

'General' Millen had been on the British payroll for twenty years and seemed the ideal person to use as a cat's paw in the scheme to bring down Parnell. Joseph Nolan, the MP whom Melville and Harkins visited at the Commons, was a crony of Parnell's and this suggested a connection between Parnell and terrorism. At the very least, it seems certain that the British Government was in some way connected with the affair that became known as the Jubilee Plot, but at this late stage, we shall probably never know the full extent of their involvement.

5

FIGHTING BACK:
THE POLITICAL POLICE
IN BRITAIN

We have seen how spies and double agents proved invaluable to the authorities in this country when dealing with the threat of terrorism in the late nineteenth century. This reliance upon the paid informer or agent provocateur was already well established by the time that the Fenians became active in the 1860s and 1870s. The practice of keeping an eye on potentially subversive political activity began in earnest during the Industrial Revolution a century earlier. The use of spies in this way actually predated the creation of police forces in this country. After the Napoleonic Wars, there was a real risk of insurrection and this was met by the government of the day infiltrating groups such as the Cato Street Conspirators in order to discover their plans.

Later on, in the early years of Victoria's reign, the Chartists were active in opposing the government. The army played a pivotal role in countering Chartist conspiracies, by encouraging off-duty soldiers to associate with factory workers and report on what was being said. Tactics of this sort proved far more effective than the overt and often brutal repression being practised in other European countries. The British Establishment seldom found it necessary to resort to brutality; they could instead break up conspiracies before they had a chance to mature into violent action. It was perhaps inevitable that when the Fenian troubles began in the late 1860s, the Cabinet thought first of counter-intelligence rather than brutal suppression. This was purely a matter of realpolitik; experience had taught the authorities that this was likely to be a more effective tactic. After the Clerkenwell explosion in 1867, some countries would have closed down newspapers and instituted mass arrests. While it is true that thousands of special constables were enrolled and sent to guard gasometers and government offices, this sort of police action was soon abandoned. The British Government had a better idea.

On Saturday 14 December 1867, the day after the Clerkenwell Outrage, Benjamin Disraeli set in motion the process of creating Britain's first secret police. He arranged for a soldier, a Guards officer called Lieutenant Colonel William Fielding, to establish a department in London which would be a cross between an army unit and a police department. Its provisional name was to be the Counter Revolutionary Secret Service Department. Colonel Fielding had been based in Dublin castle before this, where he had been very successful in fighting the Fenians on their home ground. He was, it was thought, the ideal man to lead a counter-attack on the Fenianism that was now rearing its head on the British mainland. Although it was nominally the prime minister, Lord Derby, who set up this new office, the brains behind it were Disraeli's. On 14 December, he wrote to Derby:

> I will not trouble you with all the schemes, conferences, hopes, and disappointments, of this busy day. The result is that Colonel Fielding, who has just left my room, has undertaken to ascertain, if possible, the relation between the Fenians in England and the revolutionary societies abroad …

Colonel Fielding was allocated two assistants. One was Captain Whelan, another soldier, and the other was Robert Anderson, an Irish-born lawyer who was to go on to become assistant commissioner at Scotland Yard. Two detective inspectors from the Metropolitan Police were also seconded to the newly formed section. Robert Anderson was the son of the Crown Solicitor and brother of an Attorney General. He had worked in Dublin, investigating the Fenian movement, before being summoned to London to help Colonel Fielding set up his new unit. He seemed an ideal candidate for this project, where his official title was Civilian Secretary.

From the beginning, Anderson took a robust and no-nonsense approach to matters. Soon after he had been sent to London to help with the new department, he met with a civil servant from the Home Office. To his amazement, he learned that this young man always carried a revolver with him, in case he was attacked by Fenians. More than that, many of the other private secretaries did the same. To Anderson, this seemed absolutely ludicrous; he regarded the Clerkenwell explosion as an accident and the risk of further attacks as negligible. When he first had a meeting about the Secret

Service, he was told that the plan was that the newly established group should be based in a private house in a nondescript street. This, it was felt, was the best way of keeping the whole business secret. Anderson would have none of it and insisted on being given a desk at a proper office in a government building.

Robert Anderson was an extremely honest man. In addition to being a barrister, he was also a well-known theologian; in fact he wrote no fewer than twenty-three books on theology. Rather than play along with the fears which seemed to have gripped the entire Cabinet, he attempted, not always successfully, to inject a little common sense into the question of the threat from Fenianism in Britain. There were plenty of extravagant rumours floating around London in the aftermath of the Clerkenwell Outrage: plans to blow up the Houses of Parliament, plots to use a special kind of inflammable liquid that could not be extinguished by water, a new Great Fire of London, even talk of an Irish plot to tunnel under St Paul's Cathedral and blow it up. As Robert Anderson remarked in his memoirs: 'I suppose I ought to have accepted the situation and posed as the saviour of my country; but my efforts were chiefly aimed at preventing or exploding scares. In some quarters my cynical scepticism was not appreciated.'

Anderson's role was hazy and ill defined. He was a lawyer employed by the British Government to counter a threat which he felt to be almost non-existent. The Secret Service Department did not last long, being disbanded in the same month that Michael Barrett was hanged for his part in the Clerkenwell Outrage. The disbanding of the Secret Service Department did not mean the end of Robert Anderson's career in counter-espionage, though. He stayed on at the Home Office as a special advisor and for some years ran a network of spies and informers who fed him information about the activities and plans of the Fenians in England.

The sudden wave of bombings in this country, which began with an explosion at the barracks in Manchester in 1881, took everybody by surprise. Robert Anderson's informers had known nothing of it and it was fairly obvious that the government needed a better source of intelligence than the part-time services of a theologian. It was decided to set up a dedicated section of Scotland Yard whose only task would be to fight the Irish terrorists.

It was originally planned to call this new department the Political Branch. Common sense prevailed, though, and it was realised that this name had a distinctly sinister ring to it. Instead the name 'Special Irish Branch' was agreed upon. At its formation on 17 March 1883, it had just twelve members and was headed by Chief Inspector Adolphus Williamson, who had been one of the police officers who had worked alongside Robert Anderson in 1867. Williamson was also the head of the entire CID and it was soon found to make more sense to have one officer dedicated to just the supervision of the Special Irish Branch alone. This was Inspector John Littlechild. Among his small staff of officers was an Irishman called William Melville, who was to become a legendary figure at Scotland Yard.

Theoretically, Anderson was to liaise between the Branch and the Home Office, but he was soon left out of the loop, and by 1884 his connection with counter-intelligence work had ended. The Special Irish Branch was successful from the very beginning in tracking down and deterring the extremists who were conducting the terrorist attacks. Much of this success was achieved through the use of informers.

The informer is a figure of almost mythical hatred and detestation in Irish republicanism. Not that informers and double agents are peculiar to terrorist movements. The anarchists too had their share of spies who were ready and willing to betray the machinations of their comrades to the police, usually for a price. In many of the trials held of Fenian bombers, the initial indictment often contains more names than actually appear in the dock. This was another tactic played by the Special Branch. The youngest or weakest member of the captured group would be offered immunity from prosecution if he was prepared to turn Queen's Evidence. This was vividly illustrated during the trial of the supposed Clerkenwell bombers. One of those arrested in the aftermath of the explosion, Patrick Mullaney, was not charged in connection with the attack on the prison, but held instead upon another, non-capital charge. His evidence was crucial and it was revealed that both he and another of the defendants had been offered a deal to save their necks. As one of the counsel remarked dryly at the Old Bailey: 'It must have been a dead heat as to which of you informed first.'

This is, of course, a time-honoured technique which was in use long before the Special Branch utilised it and which is still going strong today. Thus, for Irish republicans there can be only one response to the informer, traitor, double agent or volunteer who might give evidence to save his own skin; such individuals are executed as soon as they are found.

A classic example of this type of method was seen during the trail of Thomas Gallagher, Alfred Whitehead, Henry Wilson, William Ansburgh, John Curtin and Bernard Gallagher at the Old Bailey in May 1883. The men were all charged with treason felony, having 'unlawfully compassed, imagined, devised and intended to depose the Queen from the Imperial Crown of Great Britain and Ireland and expressing the same by diverse overt acts'.

During early 1883 the six men belonged to a group of seven who had come to Britain from America to plant bombs on behalf of the Clan na Gael. They were Rossa's Skirmishers, part of the widespread Fenian bombing campaign which took place during the early 1880s. The seventh member of the group was Joseph William Lynch, an Irishman who had lived in New York for many years. He had been drawn into the conspiracy by appeals to his patriotism as an Irishman. It was not until he had been provided with a ticket to England and saw what was actually being undertaken that he realised the full enormity of what was being done.

In fact, he was to be used as a courier for a group of terrorists in the Midlands who were manufacturing nitroglycerine. The amounts involved in this conspiracy, led by Thomas Gallagher, were simply vast. It involved the purchase at different times of over 3,000lb of sulphuric acid and almost 2,000lb of nitric acid. This was in addition to hundredweights of glycerine and other assorted chemicals. Lynch took fright and tipped off the police about what was happening. It was perhaps just as well that he did so. At one point the conspirators, having begun the manufacture of nitroglycerine on an industrial scale in a rented shop in Birmingham, decided that they would need to transport the finished product to London, where it could be used in a terrorist 'spectacular'. We have already seen how delicate nitroglycerine is and how carefully it must be moved from place to place. In an act of almost unbelievable folly, the terrorists decided to transfer the explosives by train from Birmingham to London, filling up rubber fisherman's waders with the deadly and unstable liquid, which were then treated like any other piece of luggage. In this way, over 400lb of the deadly high explosive were carried on an ordinary express train full of passengers. It is a miracle that no harm befell anybody as the result of these activities.

Lynch's information gave the Special Irish Branch the lead which they needed in order to roll up the whole network. By allowing him to plead Queen's Evidence, he was granted immunity from prosecution and his evidence resulted in the whole gang being sent to prison for life.

It was because of the magnitude of the threat posed by major conspiracies like that of Thomas Gallagher and his gang that it was thought perfectly justifiable to recruit double agents and even plant informers in terrorist groups, whether anarchists or Fenians. There is one very serious problem, though, which intelligence work of this kind must guard against. When even those at the top of such groups are likely to find that trusted colleagues are working for the police, to what extent might the police themselves be implicated in planned attacks? Indeed, the suggestion was more than once made in the early days of the Special Branch that it was the police themselves, via their double agents, who were actually instigating the terrorist acts that they were claiming to be detecting and preventing. We saw this accusation being made in connection with the Walsall anarchist bomb plot by a former sergeant from the Special Branch after he had been sacked. We also saw that the brother-in-law of Bourdin, the bomber killed at the Greenwich Observatory, was in the pay of the police. The theme of Joseph Conrad's novel *The Secret Agent* is that the attack at Greenwich was set up by an agent provocateur. It is at least odd that in real life Bourdin's brother should have been a prominent anarchist, editor of a magazine that called for terrorist attacks and was at the same time taking money from the Special Branch in order to keep them informed about anarchist activity in London.

During the Fenian dynamiters' campaign, the Special Irish Branch more than proved their value. So much so, that after the end of the bombings, some of which might have been precipitated by officers from the Branch, it was decided not to disband them. As Sir John Moylens remarked in his book about Scotland Yard, 'Once the Special Branch had been established, there was no lack of work for it'. In 1888, the word 'Irish' was dropped and from then on it was known simply as the Special Branch.

During the anarchist activities of the 1880s and 1890s, the Special Branch was most effective at penetrating groups planning attacks in this country. Most plans, such as those of the Wallsall anarchists, were nipped in the bud. Almost invariably, such groups were infiltrated by Special Branch spies and informers. Had this not been the case, then Britain too would probably have suffered more serious attacks, such as those in France and Spain. Despite its useful work, the Special Branch remained a very small outfit, numbering no more than twenty officers by the turn of the century.

Returning to the idea that the police themselves may have been behind some of the planned attacks by Fenians and anarchists, it is impossible today to be sure what was happening at that time. There can be no doubt that individual police officers had powerful motives for exaggerating the scale of the threat from terrorism. Let us take one police officer and see how the menace of terrorism worked to his advantage.

William Melville was born in Ireland in 1850. He came to London and at the age of 22 joined the Metropolitan Police. In 1879, when he was not yet 30, he was promoted to sergeant and four years later he was seconded to the newly formed Special Irish Branch. He was posted to the French port of Le Havre the following year, where he watched those embarking for England. In 1887, he was involved in investigating the so-called Jubilee Plot, a key figure of which was a paid agent of the British police. So far, William Melville's career was one of steady and slow application. Suddenly, it took off meteorically and within a few short years William Melville was one of the best-known men in England. The catalyst for this sudden celebrity was the Walsall anarchist plot, which he was apparently instrumental in disrupting.

We cannot now know the full extent and nature of Detective Inspector Melville's relationship with Auguste Coulon, the key figure in the Walsall plot, but it is certainly a fact that Coulon was in the pay of the police and acting on their behalf. At the trial, it was alleged that the bomb casings around which the entire case hinged would never have been produced in the first place without Coulon's active encouragement and practical help. The suspicion that the Walsall plot was engineered by the police them-selves and, more specifically, that it was the brainchild of William Melville, appeared in an anarchist magazine soon after those involved had been sent to prison. The *Commonweal* published an article which said:

> The Walsall Anarchists have been condemned – Charles, Battola, and Cailes to ten years' penal servitude, while Deakin has been let off in mercy with five. For what? For a police plot concocted by one of those infamous wretches who make a living by getting up these affairs and selling their victims to the vengeance of the law.

Essentially, the writer was setting out the theory that the police themselves had been behind the whole so-called plot. Had he stopped here, he might have got away with it, but he went on to name names and it was this which landed him in the dock at the Old Bailey on a charge of seditious libel. He continued: 'What of the spy Melville, who sets his agent on to concoct the plots which he discovers? Are these men fit to live?'

David Nicoll, editor of *Commonweal* and author of the offending article, had also made speeches in which he called for the deaths of the Home Secretary and the judge who had sent the Walsall plotters to prison. On 2 May 1892, he stood trial charged with 'inciting, soliciting, and encouraging certain persons unknown to murder the Right Hon. Henry Matthews, Secretary of State for the Home Department; Sir Henry Hawkins, one of the Justices of the High Court of Justice; and William Melville, inspector of police'.

It was not that long since Johann Most had been sent to prison for precisely the same offence and David Nicoll ended up being sent to prison for eighteen months. Even today, inciting the murder of the Home Secretary is liable to bring you to the attention of the police and it is a measure of the seriousness with which this was viewed that the Attorney General prosecuted the case in person. It was clear during the trial that rumours were even then floating about as to the extent to which the police themselves had been involved in the Walsall affair and that the editor of *Commonweal* had simply been printing what others were saying on the street.

It is very strange to see the way that this one officer always seemed to be on the scene and in the thick of things, even when off duty. Take the truly extraordinary circumstances surrounding the arrest of Théodule Meunier, for instance. This French anarchist was wanted in his own country for several bombings, including one in a cafe where a man was killed. He fled to London and remained here for some time as a refugee. The French badly wanted to try him and asked the British police to keep an eye out for him. According to the official version, Detective Inspector Melville just happened to be on the platform at Victoria station on 4 April 1894, when who should he spot standing next to him? None other than the wanted man himself. Melville supposedly arrested the man single-handedly and took him to the nearest police station. Meunier was extradited to France a couple of months later and sent to prison for life.

One can easily see that a smart and ambitious man on the make like Melville would have every motive for inciting plots via informers and then apparently breaking up terrorist cells by his formidable powers of detection. His career certainly flourished as a result of the anarchist and Fenian threats.

William Melville's career with the police brings us to the other arm of the state in combating subversion and terrorism: the security service, more commonly known as MI5. There was, until the early years of the twentieth century, no clear demarcation between the police and the army when it came to dealing with domestic unrest. High-ranking army officers encouraged their men to spy on and report on the activities of civilian malcontents whom they met in the pubs of garrison towns. The army were called on to assist the civil power fairly regularly in the decades leading up to the First World War and quite a few senior police officers, even including commissioners of police for the metropolis, were drawn from the ranks of the army. When 'Melville of the Yard' suddenly and unexpectedly retired in 1903 at the relatively young age of 53, there was widespread speculation as to why England's most famous police officer should suddenly have given up his job. The explanation was a simple one. Just as army officers drifted into police work, so too did the process work in the opposite direction.

In 19c3, the War Office set up a Directorate of Military Operations. They wished for this to be run by a senior detective and Melville fitted the bill perfectly. His reputation for thwarting plots to blow up the queen or bomb London stood him in good stead and he was a natural choice for the controller of this new government department. In 1909, Melville's post was incorporated into the newly formed MI5, where he stayed until his retirement. When Melville was running agents for the Directorate of Military Operations, he was referred to for security reasons by the initial letter of his surname, 'M'. This became something of a tradition which was noted by Ian Fleming and used in his James Bond books, where James Bond's superior goes by the soubriquet 'M'.

The problem with all counter-revolutionary police and army units is that they owe their very existence to threats of violence from which they alone can protect society. Unless the Special Branch or MI5 are constantly uncovering new plots and menaces to public security, then questions will be asked about the need for them. It is worth recalling Robert Anderson's statement above, that: 'I suppose I ought to have accepted the situation and posed as the saviour of my country; but my efforts were chiefly aimed at preventing or exploding scares. In some quarters my cynical scepticism was not appreciated.'

The truth is that a hundred years ago, as now, the Special Branch needed desperately to persuade both the government and the general population that they faced unparalleled dangers. If they failed to do this, then the unit runs the risk of having its funding slashed or even being done away with altogether.

This then is the danger when special units are supposedly fighting subversion and terrorism. The aims and purposes of both terrorists and police officers coincide dangerously and they often seem to be playing a double-handed game between themselves.

Attempts by the government and police to prevent or deter terrorist attacks can backfire in other ways and produce the very things which it is hoped to avoid. In 1884, two 24-year-old men, William Woolf and Edward Bondurand, appeared at the Old Bailey charged under the Explosive

Substances Act, which had been passed the previous year in the wake of the Fenian dynamite outrages. The allegation was that they had had in their possession a quantity of explosives, which they were intending to use to blow up the German embassy in London. The Home Secretary had offered very large rewards to anybody giving information leading to the arrest and conviction of terrorist bombers. This move had been motivated by the Irish attacks in London.

As the trial of Woolf and Bondurand progressed, it gradually became apparent that things were not as they had at first appeared. The aim of the whole plot, in which the two accused men were probably involved, had been to obtain the £1,000 reward. Fifteen pounds of gunpowder had been bought and not one but two police informers were mixed up in the business. There was also reference to a police officer who had allegedly helped arrange things. In the event, the jury retired for nearly six hours without being able to reach a verdict and the case was quietly dropped.

6

THE TOTTENHAM OUTRAGE

A wages snatch goes disastrously wrong. The robbers, asylum seekers trying to raise funds for a terrorist group, gun down a policeman and a passing child. Police and passers-by pursue them as they hijack a succession of getaway vehicles. Over 200 shots are fired, two people killed and nineteen wounded by gunfire, before the chase ends with a siege by armed police. It's a scenario which could have come from today's headlines, almost anywhere in the world. Incredible as it may seem, it all happened in London over a hundred years ago.

When Police Constable Sharon Beshenivsky was shot dead by Somali asylum seekers who were carrying out an armed robbery in 2005, it was seen by many as a shocking example of the dangerous times in which we live. After all, things didn't used to be like this, did they? Reckless foreign gangsters shooting down an unarmed police officer in this way; nothing like this had ever been seen before in this country. Since the perpetrators of the crime were African refugees, many people in this country connected the tragic event with the large numbers of asylum seekers who had been entering the country in recent years. The news that one of the killers fled the country on his sister's passport while wearing a burqa did not help matters. Ruthless killings of this sort have, over the last decade or so, become associated in the public mind with foreign-born criminals, typified by the Yardie gangsters of London. Such ideas are nothing new.

As the first decade of the twentieth century was ending, there was a distinct feeling amongst many people in Britain that the country was full. It was chiefly full up with Eastern European asylum seekers, thousands of whom were still entering the country each year. As we shall later see, exactly the

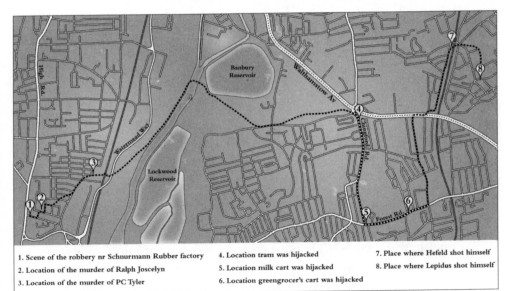

1. Scene of the robbery nr Schnurmann Rubber factory
2. Location of the murder of Ralph Joscelyn
3. Location of the murder of PC Tyler
4. Location tram was hijacked
5. Location milk cart was hijacked
6. Location greengrocer's cart was hijacked
7. Place where Hefeld shot himself
8. Place where Lepidus shot himself

The Tottenham Outrage – the route taken by escaping bandits.

same verbal gymnastics were being performed by home secretaries being questioned about immigration statistics as are seen today during questions in the House of Commons. In fact, around half a million foreigners a year were entering England in 1910. True, many people were also leaving the country, but there was still what we call today a net inflow of refugees and asylum seekers running into hundreds of thousands a year.

By the time of President McKinley's assassination by a Polish anarchist in 1901, the anarchist scare in this country was dying down a little. The primary concerns about foreigners coming into this country in the early years of the century had less to do with the possibility that they were terrorists and more to do with the fear that they would deprive British people of jobs, houses and school places, and at the same time probably becoming involved in criminal activity. In the latter half of the nineteenth century, upwards of 150,000 Jews settled in this country. They were all from Eastern Europe and Russia. These concerns led in 1905 to the passing of the first ever restrictions on immigration into this country. Up until that time, as A.J.P. Taylor remarked, 'a foreigner could spend his life in this country without permit and without informing the police'.

In the first few years of the twentieth century, thousands of asylum seekers from Russia and Eastern Europe entered this country. As one might expect, these newcomers tended to cluster together for security, with the inevitable result that some districts began to take on the appearance of ghettoes. In London, many of the immigrants were Jewish and they tended to congregate in that part of London where the French Protestant refugees had settled a century or more earlier, Whitechapel and Stepney. Like the earlier immigrants to that area, many of them took up making and repairing clothes; it was estimated that 10 per cent of these newcomers worked as tailors.

The complaints about these refugees and asylum seekers will have a very familiar sound to modern readers. In 1902 the MP for one of the districts most affected by immigration, Stepney, rose to make a speech in the House of Commons. Major William Evans-Gordon was furious. He claimed that in some schools 'Few English pupils are to be found'. He went on to complain that there was a housing crisis, with ordinary people in his constituency being 'ruthlessly turned out to make room for foreign invaders'. These immigrants were, he asserted, bringing crime to the areas in which they lived and many of them were suffering from contagious diseases.

The same year that Major Evans-Gordon made his speech in Parliament, a pressure group was founded in London called the British Brotherhood. Their slogan was 'England for the English' and they were opposed not only to immigration, but also to the import of cheaply manufactured foreign goods which were seen as a threat to the livelihood of British workers. It was not only extremists such as the members of the British Brotherhood who were agitated by the issue of immigration. Ordinary workers, too, were angry about the numbers of foreigners who were flocking to this country. It was suggested that we in England were taking more than our share of these asylum seekers and that other Western European countries were not doing enough. One concern, which will be immediately recognised by readers today, was the idea that the immigrants were placing a terrible burden on local authorities. They did not really want to work at all and expected to be kept by the state. Another wholly contradictory claim was being made at the same time. It was that Eastern European workers were taking the jobs away from English workers by working for lower wages. Pressure increased on the government until they announced the setting up of a Royal Commission on aliens, the commonest expression then used for foreigners, which would look into the whole question of immigration and asylum seekers.

When the Royal Commission released its findings in 1903, it was quickly discovered that almost all the fears which had been expressed were completely groundless. In fact, Britain was taking fewer, not more refugees than other countries in Europe. Those coming here were grateful for the opportunity to start afresh and worked hard. The crime rate was no higher among the immigrant population than it was anywhere else in the country and as for the idea that they were sponging on the state, the Commission found that in fact only 1 per cent of such families were in receipt of Poor Law payments.

One might have supposed that after discovering that there was nothing to worry about, the Royal Commission would have left it at that, but they did not. In defiance of all the evidence that they had so painstakingly collected, the Commission recommended controls on immigration, the first restrictions to be imposed upon those entering the country in British history. For the increasingly unpopular Conservative government led by Arthur Balfour, the fuss about immigration and the recommendations about new legislation to control it gave them the opportunity for a shamelessly populist bit of grandstanding.

The Aliens Act 1905 set out to limit immigration into this country. It was passed despite the Labour MP Kier Hardy assuring the House that there was no demand for it among the working classes whom he represented. There had been calls for an annual quota or 'cap' on immigration, of the sort to which the present coalition is committed. This did not, however, find its way into the act. The main provisions were that a body of officers was established who had the power to refuse entry to 'undesirable' immigrants – a kind of Edwardian border police. They would keep a particular eye out for those with no visible means of support. There were two important clauses of the act which meant that the flow of refugees and asylum seekers was unlikely to be stemmed by it. Anybody who was fleeing persecution or ill treatment on religious or political grounds was exempted from the provisions of the 1905 Act. An appeals tribunal was also set up so that those refused entry or scheduled to be deported could have a chance to plead their case. Once again, the twenty-first-century reader will perhaps be thinking that this all sounds very modern.

In many ways, early twentieth-century Britain was very similar to early twenty-first-century Britain. The Edwardian era, like our own, was in the grip of an information revolution. Telephones and typewriters were becoming common, as were gramophones. The box brownie appeared on the scene in 1900, a camera so cheap, robust and easy to use that a child could be given it. Exciting new technology made its appearance in this decade. Wireless telegraphy, for example, made it possible to keep in touch with a ship in the middle of the Atlantic Ocean, an almost unimaginable achievement even for the late Victorians. The first aeroplane made its flight in 1903 and, by 1909, Bleriot had flown across the Channel in one. All in all, this was a decade of great change for the country. Such periods of rapid change can be very unsettling for those who live through them. Throw into this a wave of uncontrolled and seemingly unlimited immigration and it is hardly to be wondered at that some people felt a little unsettled and even vaguely threatened.

The 1905 Aliens Act was not, in the end, very effective at preventing undesirables from coming to Britain. It was said that the flow of immigrants into the country was reduced by about 30 to 40 per cent, but others doubted this. It is quite true that then, as now, the majority of those seeking sanctuary in this country were ordinary families who wished simply to live and work quietly, grateful for the opportunities which this country afforded them. Nevertheless, among these hardworking and law abiding people was a scattering of dangerous criminals and dedicated terrorists, and the actions of such individuals tended to reflect badly upon other immigrants. Men such as Paul Hefeld and Jacob Lepidus, who had grown up together in the Baltic port of Riga. They were both anarchists who had been deeply involved in the revolutionary movement in Russia and, after the abortive Russian Revolution of 1905, they fled to England.

The modern-day independent Baltic states of Latvia, Lithuania and Estonia did not exist before the end of the First World War. Up until that time they were no more than minor provinces of the Russian Empire. They were home, though, to a very fierce independence movement, which contained many Jewish anarchists. Paul Hefeld and Jacob Lepidus were among them. In a later chapter we shall make the acquaintance of more Jewish anarchists and they too came from Latvia.

After arriving in England, Hefeld and Lepidus joined the community of expatriate Russians living in the East End of London. There they helped in the printing of seditious leaflets, which were smuggled into Russia, and there is some evidence that they also became involved in the manufacture of bombs, which were also sent to Russia. These activities were expensive and by the end of 1908 the political group to which they were affiliated was running desperately short of funds.

For a time, Hefeld had worked at the Schnurmann rubber factory in Tottenham, a suburb in north London. Districts which have a high number of immigrants of one type often attract other immigrants in later years, who typically displace the original inhabitants. Sometimes these communities are very different from those which went before. The classic example of this is the Brick Lane area of Whitechapel. In the late eighteenth and early nineteenth centuries, Brick Lane was famous for the large number of French refugees living and working there. A century later and they had been replaced by Jews from Russia and Eastern Europe. Today Brick Lane has neither French Protestants nor Jews. Instead, it is known as a centre for Bangladeshi Muslims. The nearby church, first used for French services, was later converted into a synagogue. It is now a mosque. A similar process has taken place in Tottenham. A hundred years ago, the part of Tottenham near the White Hart Lane stadium was known as 'Little Russia' because of the large number of Russian Jews living there. It is for this reason that the Tottenham Hotspur football team are know colloquially as 'the Yids' to this very day. Tottenham is now noted for the numbers of Caribbean and Africans living there and the old synagogues of the Russian Jews have been converted to Pentecostal churches.

Hefeld and Lepidus were therefore familiar with Tottenham and thought it a suitable place to stage a daring and audacious robbery. In addition to smuggling propaganda into Russia, the two men were almost certainly also involved in gunrunning. They borrowed a couple of automatic pistols from a consignment headed for their homeland and, their pockets sagging with cartridges, travelled one morning to Tottenham.

Saturday was payday at the Schnurmann's factory. The wages, about £80 in gold and silver, were brought by car from a bank in Hackney. Saturday 23 January 1909 began like any other day at the rubber factory in Chesnut Road, just off the High Road. The men worked steadily through the morning, waiting for lunchtime when they got their wages. At 11.50 a.m. a car pulled up outside the factory and a young clerk climbed out, clutching the leather Gladstone bag containing the money. Immediately, two men rushed up, knocked him down and made off with the bag. Alerted by the clerk's shouts, several of the men from the factory ran out and gave chase. At the corner of the street the robbers turned and opened fire with their pistols, wounding one man and causing the others to dive for cover.

The sound of gunfire brought three policemen running from the police station in Tottenham High Road and, seeing that the men were racing towards Tottenham Marshes, Constables Tyler and Williams ran to head them off. A third policeman commandeered the firm's car, ordering the driver to follow the bandits, who had now run as far as the neighbouring Scales road. As the car turned into the street, it was blasted by bullets, which shattered the windscreen and radiator. Ten-year-old Ralph Joscelyn ran out of his house to see what all the noise was about and was instantly shot dead.

As the gunmen reached the railway line, on the other side of which lay the marshes, Williams and Tyler confronted them. PC Tyler called upon them to surrender. Without hesitating, one of the men shot him through the head, while his companion fired a couple of bullets at Williams. The robbers then climbed a fence and ran across the marshes towards Banbury reservoir, skirted the southern edge of it, then ran south towards Walthamstow. Perhaps they thought that they had frightened off their pursuers, but if so, they were gravely mistaken.

The cold-blooded murders of little Ralph Joscelyn and PC Tyler had transformed the crowd of factory hands and local residents into something approaching a lynch mob. This was largely farming land in 1909 and so there were plenty of shotguns in circulation. A number of men armed themselves and followed the killers. The police too lost no time in breaking open the locked cupboard at the police station containing firearms and to which nobody apparently had a key. The revolvers inside were swiftly issued to any available police officer. Tottenham police station also had a supply of cutlasses which were at one time standard issue to some forces. Some of these were also handed out and a couple of men set off on bicycles waving cutlasses. This is believed to be the last time that British police ever used these weapons in action. It was accordingly a large and pretty heavily armed crowd which finally caught up with Hefeld and Lapidus in the fields north of Billet Road in Walthamstow.

A running gun battle developed as the posse on foot, bicycle and horseback exchanged shots with the desperados. Some of the crowd were wounded, but this only increased the anger and determination of the others to capture them. Eventually the two men scrambled over a fence and found themselves in Chingford Road. A tram came into view and at once they began firing at it in order to bring it to a halt. The driver very nimbly climbed up on to the roof and so the conductor was marched to the front and ordered to drive it. A passenger unwise enough to protest was promptly shot. The tram rumbled south, Hefeld holding a gun to the conductor's head while Jacob Lepidus fired at the pursuers. When they reached Forest Road, the men abandoned the tram and seized a horse-drawn milk float. The milkman was left lying in the road with a bullet in his chest.

They drove off at such a furious pace that the van overturned after a travelling a hundred yards or so. Without wasting any time, they switched vehicles to a greengrocer's horse and cart. Seeing a policeman on point duty, one of the men shot at him as they drove past. Hardly able to believe his eyes, PC Adams stopped a motorist, climbed into his car and ordered him to follow the horse and cart, maintaining a safe distance.

By this time police from Tottenham, accompanied by a band of vigilantes, had once again picked up the trail. The greengrocer's cart overturned when Hefeld and Lepidus attempted to turn a corner at speed, so they continued on foot. Now they were once again heading north, in the general direction of Hale End. Although running for their lives, the two men were absolutely exhausted, having been on the run continuously for more than two hours. They managed to struggle on for another mile until they reached the River Ching, at the point where it flows under a railway viaduct just south of Highams Park station. Hefeld could run no further. He sank wearily down on the riverbank, reloaded his pistol and carried on firing until he ran out of ammunition. The pursuers closed in and Hefledt either shot himself or was shot by one of the infuriated mob.

Meanwhile, Lepidus had crossed the railway and was nearing the edge of Epping Forest. Standing alone at the very edge of the forest was a tiny rustic cottage, occupied by Charles Rolston, a coalman, and his family. Lepidus kicked the front door open and wordlessly crashed up the stairs. Smashing a window in the bedroom, he began firing his last few cartridges at the grim and purposeful men who had followed him this far and who now surrounded the cottage. Rolston had grabbed his family and hurried them out of the house at the first sound of gunfire, so Lepidus was entirely alone.

When the firing died down, PC Charles Eagles and a detective called Dixon rushed into the cottage and kicked down the door of the room in which Lepidus was hiding. He had saved the last bullet for himself and lay dead on the floor. There were sooty hand marks around the chimney breast, which suggested to the police that, even at the last moment, Lepidus thought that he might be able to escape by climbing up the chimney. They didn't investigate the chimney closely, though, and local legend has it that the wages bag containing £80 was stuffed up there and that the Rolston family lived quite comfortably on this for some time afterwards. At any rate, the bag of money was never found and this story seems as likely as any to account for its disappearance.

Hefeld had not died by the bank of the River Ching, although he was very badly hurt. He died a week later, under police guard in the Prince of Wales Hospital in Tottenham. His last words were, 'My mother is in Riga.'

This then was the extraordinary affair which became known as the Tottenham Outrage. There was an unprecedented surge of popular indignation against foreign immigrants. Many demonstrated their feelings by attending the funeral of PC Tyler. His funeral signalled the same kind of public disapproval of murders of this sort, much in the same way Sergeant Brett's did forty years earlier.

The combined funerals of Ralph Joscelyn and PC Tyler took place on Friday 29 January. There have probably never been funerals quite like these in England, either before or since. The two corteges started off separately and then joined together in Tottenham High Road. The Commissioner of Police, Sir Edward Henry, was there, as was an MP representing the Home Secretary. The procession was led by the police band, which played the dead march as it passed Tottenham police station, which was draped in black, and then moved on past the parades of shops. Every single shop was closed and their shutters also draped in black, as was the railway bridge at Stamford Hill, under which the cortege passed. It was an amazing sight. There were mounted police, 200 police marching on foot, a platoon of the Scots Guards, a troop of Royal Artillery, contingents of tram drivers, postmen and council workers. The immense crowds had come from all over London, with an estimated half a million mourners lining the streets to Abney Park cemetery in Stoke Newington. Today, PC Tyler's grave is marked by an extraordinary marble monument which includes a sculpted replica of his helmet and cape, complete with his police number. Little Ralph Joscelyn lies nearby in a slightly more modest but still well-tended plot.

The aftermath of the Tottenham Outrage contains a few points of interest. To begin with, there was a great increase in anti-Semitism across Britain, but especially in London. Here was a community which sheltered the most desperate criminals, whose ruthless behaviour was so different from anything seen before in this country. What particularly angered people was that the community to which he belonged had been allowed to enter the country in order to escape persecution. This sort of behaviour seemed poor repayment for such hospitality. Irrational as it was, the conduct of the two men was thought to reflect poorly upon all the other hundreds of thousand of refugees and asylum seekers from Eastern Europe who had come to live here. Precisely the same kind of unreasoning fury may be observed today when a member of such a community commits an especially atrocious crime.

It was suddenly realised after the Tottenham Outrage that there was no suitable award for bravery among the police. This was a strange oversight and it took an incident like this to bring home to everybody that no matter how brave and courageous an officer was on duty, there was no decoration which he could be awarded. The King's Police Medal was instituted by Edward VII in July of that year.

Another curious thing is that we talk today of the 'Compensation Culture' as though it is something novel, a new development. It is not. Following the Tottenham Outrage, word leaked out that a fund was available to compensate anybody who had suffered as a result of the incident. There was a flood of claims, many of them plainly spurious: damages to clothing and property, even a claim for financial compensation for the stress and alarm experienced just by witnessing the chase.

We act as though the use of firearms is a disturbing new phenomenon and that there was once a time when nobody in this country ever got shot by crazed gunmen. It is not really true. There never was a time when dangerous and violent criminals did not pursue their goals with reckless disregard for the lives of others. We see it today and it was the case a century ago. Two years after the Tottenham Outrage there was another case of police officers being murdered by asylum seekers. This crime was far worse than that committed at Tottenham. Like the Tottenham Outrage, it has been almost completely forgotten.

7

THE HOUNDSDITCH
MURDERS AND THE
BATTLE OF STEPNEY

The murders that took place during the Tottenham Outrage caused a great deal of anger among ordinary Londoners. However irrational such a feeling may have been, the general consensus was that we had given refuge to large numbers of foreign Jews and this is how they repaid our hospitality. The fact that the affair at Tottenham involved just two men out of the thousands who had sought asylum in this country was irrelevant to popular sentiment. It came to symbolise a certain attitude felt by many people. Even if the Tottenham Outrage was a rare event, the fact was that parts of the country were now becoming crowded with refugees and asylum seekers. There simply wasn't room on this small island for all those who wished to come here from the rest of the world. Such notions have, for well over a century, been found when the discussion turns to refugees and asylum seekers in Britain.

These resentments in many of the native-born population bubbled away over the next couple of years following the Tottenham Outrage. Then, almost exactly two years later, occurred a sequence of crimes which caused this latent xenophobia and anti-Semitism to erupt again. Once again, it was asylum seekers from Eastern Europe who were in the thick of it.

On the night of 16 December 1910, Max Weill, a shopkeeper in Houndsditch, a street in the City of London, heard strange noises coming from the next-door jeweller's shop. He went to the party wall and listened carefully. It sounded very much as though somebody was using a hammer and chisel to break down brickwork. It was almost ten o'clock at night, which struck the man as a strange time to be carrying out building work. He went out into the street and found the beat officer patrolling that area, a constable called Piper. He told the young officer of his suspicions, that some-body was attempting to break into the jeweller's shop. PC Piper fetched a sergeant from Bishopsgate police station and they went into Weill's shop to listen to the sounds. The sergeant, Bentley, sent PC Piper round at once to the back of the jeweller's shop to see what was going on. In Cutler Street there was row of houses which backed on to the shops in Houndsditch. It was called Exchange Buildings and number eleven was right behind the jewellers in Houndsditch.

PC Piper knocked on the door and when a man answered, he asked what all the noise was about. Something about the man's behaviour roused the liveliest suspicions in the young policeman's mind and he simply left at once, an action which almost certainly saved his life. He went straight back to the sergeant and told him that there was something very fishy going on. At this stage, the worst that the police could possibly have been expect-ing was to interrupt a burglary in progress. They decided in any case to make sure that there were enough of them to deal with any trouble. They returned to the police station for reinforcements.

At Bishopsgate police station they collected another seven officers, two of them sergeants. When they returned to the shop, there seemed to be no sign of anything untoward and so PC Piper was left to stand guard there while the other officers went round the back into Cutler Street. Exchange Buildings was in a narrow cul-de-sac leading off Cutler Street. They then began knocking on all the doors to see if they could find anybody who could explain what all the noise was about. Sergeants Bentley and Bryant ended up knocking on the front door of No 11 Exchange Buildings, the door at which PC Piper had already knocked a few minutes earlier. It proved to be a mistake, because the occupants of the house were already forewarned and indeed forearmed.

The door was opened almost immediately by a foreign-looking indi-vidual who was evidently unable to understand the questions that the two sergeants were asking.

'Is anybody working out the back?' asked Sergeant Bentley. 'Do you mind if we have a look?'

The man indicated that they should wait on the doorstep. He pushed the door to, without closing it entirely, leaving the police officers with the impression that he had gone to fetch somebody who spoke English. The plan of these houses was that the whole of the ground floor was taken up by a single room, from which a staircase led to the upper storeys. Directly opposite the front door was a back door which led to an open yard. It was here that access could be gained to the rear wall of the jeweller's shop.

After waiting for a minute or so, Sergeant Bentley grew impatient. He pushed open the front door and entered the house. On the table in front of him was an oxyacetylene torch. At once, he became aware of a man standing on the staircase to his left. He called up to this shadowy and indistinct figure, 'Has anybody been working out the back? Can we go and have a look?'

The man on the stairs replied, 'In there.'

As Sergeant Bentley walked further into the room a man entered the room from the rear yard. He said nothing, but began firing at the officer with a pistol he was holding. At the same moment, the man on the stairs also began shooting. Sergeant Bentley collapsed on the threshold of the front door, shot in the face, shoulder and neck. Sergeant Bryant, although wounded, managed to stagger out of sight of the gunmen.

Hearing the fusillade of shots coming from inside the house, a constable called Woodhams ran to help Sergeant Bentley. He was at once cut down himself by gunfire, a bullet shattering his thighbone. Another sergeant called Tucker also ran to the assistance of the wounded men, before also being shot in his turn. A bullet passed straight through his heart and he was killed on the spot. At this point, the door to the house next to No 11 burst open and a man and woman ran out. This man was also armed.

None of the police had the remotest idea how to deal with this turn of events. They had gone to investigate a report of possible burglary and were now being cut down by a hail of gunfire. Before they had had a chance to collect their wits and consider the best course of action, the two men in the house at No 11 also stormed out, still firing, and tried to run clear of the cul-de-sac. One of them was grabbed by a courageous officer called Choat. There was more firing and both Choat and the man whom he had grabbed fell to the ground. PC Choat was hit by eight bullets. A ninth hit the man with whom he was struggling. When the gang finally made off, they left behind them one dead police officer, two others who would die within a day and two men who had been crippled for life. The whole dreadful business had taken less than a minute.

The police reaction to the murder of one of their own colleagues has not changed substantially over the years. They are furiously angry and will not rest until the killer is brought to justice. They also make life very difficult for anybody whom they feel capable of shedding any light on the matter and who is apparently not co-operating fully. In practice, this means raids, the chivvying about of various petty criminals and giving the general impression to everybody in the underworld that normal business will not be resumed until information leading to an arrest is forthcoming. This makes life tricky for ordinary criminals and the result is that a tip-off in these cases is often received, not in order to gain a reward, but simply so that the everyday business of petty crime can continue without constant interruption from the police.

In this case, the police had a very strong lead within twelve hours of the killings. At 3.30 a.m., Dr James Scanlan, who had a medical practice in the Commercial Road and lived above his surgery, was woken by a furious knocking on his front door. Two foreign women were on the doorstep and begged him to come at once to tend to a man whom they claimed was very badly hurt. Dr Scanlan asked why they had not taken the man to the nearby London Hospital, but they told him that the man was too badly injured to move. He went with them to 59 Grove Street, a house divided up into flats. Here, he was led into a room where a man lay on the bed. He was fully dressed and bleeding heavily from a bullet wound. The women gave him no clear explanation of how it had happened, but when he examined the man, he found that he had been shot in the back. Dr Scanlan made him as comfortable as could be expected. He went home and in the morning notified the police of the case. When he returned to Grove Street, he found that the man had died during the night.

The police secured the premises and arrested a woman they found in the room with the dead man. It was established that his name was George Gardstein and he was a Latvian Jew. It did not take them long to arrest two more men, one of whom knocked on the door asking for Gardstein. In this way, Zurka Dubof and Jacob Peters were arrested. They too were Jewish asylum seekers from the Baltic state of Latvia. The police were making good progress with their investigations. However, they also knew that some of the gang were still missing.

The woman whom they had arrested was called Nina Vassileva. She shared the flat with George Gardstein and his cousin, Fritz Svaars. A third man had seemingly lodged at the flat from time to time. The focus of the police hunt was upon this mysterious character known as Peter the Painter. This nickname had been bestowed upon him because he had relied upon house painting in the past to keep himself. His real name was supposedly Peter Piatkow. There seems to be, in retrospect, some doubt as to the very existence of Peter the Painter. Nevertheless, in the days following the

Houndsditch massacre, it was for Peter the Painter and Fritz Svaars that the police were searching.

Peter the Painter has become a legendary figure in the mythology of the East End. There has always been a fairly strong anti-police sentiment among working-class people in this part of London and the murder of three policemen in this way became celebrated in some circles. Much the same thing happened after the Shepherds Bush police murders in 1966, when three unarmed officers were gunned down by criminals. The name of the leader of the gang on that occasion, Harry Roberts, has also passed into folklore, being used as a chant used to taunt the police: 'Harry Roberts is our friend, he kills coppers'. Much the same happened with Peter the Painter.

Various tall stories have grown up about Peter the Painter over the century or so since the Siege of Sidney Street. One of the more ludicrous, based upon the broad and luxuriant moustache supposedly sported by the wanted man, is that he was actually none other than Stalin, future dictator of Soviet Russia. A more serious idea was mooted in Richard Deacon's *A History of the Secret Service*, published in 1969. The idea floated here is that Peter the Painter was an agent of the *Ochrana*, the tsarist secret police, and that he had been dispatched to this country with the aim of stirring up mischief among the anarchists in London, many of whom were exiles from the Russian Empire. According to this theory, Peter the Painter's task was to provoke the anarchists into committing outrageous and antisocial acts, so that the British would become fed up with their country being used as a refuge by such people.

This is a plausible theory, judging by what we have so far seen of the role of the double agent and agent provocateur in the affairs of terrorist movements in this country during the late nineteenth and early twentieth centuries. A shocking outrage like the Houndsditch murders would certainly have suited the Russians. It was likely to have the effect of making the British far less tolerant of the refugees and asylum seekers in their midst. In short, Russian revolutionaries might be deported back to their country of origin, where they could then be arrested and imprisoned.

A week after the murders, the funerals of the three dead police officers were held. The funeral of PC Tyler had been a grand affair, but the service for Sergeants Tucker and Bentley and Constable Choat was also impressive. For the first time in its history, St Paul's Cathedral was used to commemorate the lives of ordinary public servants. Following the service, the men were buried at Ilford cemetery.

Over the Christmas period, the police raided clubs and various properties occupied by members of the expatriate Russian and Baltic community. It was made pretty clear in the East End that this pressure would continue unabated until the remaining members of the gang who had shot down the three defenceless officers were in custody.

On 1 January 1911, these tactics paid off and the police got the break they had been looking for. That evening, Charles Perelman walked into the City of London police headquarters and announced that he knew where they could find the Houndsditch police killers. Or, to be more precise, he knew where Fritz Svaars was hiding out. Interest in Perelman's story and gratitude for his public-spirited action in coming to inform the police about this was tempered by the belief that Charles Perelman's hands might not be entirely clean. Although working as a photographer, he had connections in the anarchist community and had at one time been the landlord of one of the men whom he was now about to betray. In short, there was probably a good deal of self-interest involved in his making this statement and he probably hoped that by doing it any role of his own in the Houndsditch affair might escape notice. Although he was clearly not one of the assassins, the police rather suspected him of being a 'fence', a receiver of stolen property. It is by no means impossible that he was the man who would have been helping to dispose of the £7,000 of jewellery, if the raid on H.S. Harris' jeweller's shop had been successful.

Nevertheless, the police listened carefully as he told them that a woman called Betsy Gershon had come to him seeking help. She currently had two men staying in her flat who were on the run from the police. One of the men had given Perelman's name and address to Gershon and told her that he would help them. Instead, for reasons best known to himself, he had come straight to the police.

The two men staying with Gershon at 100 Sidney Street were William Sokoloff and Fritz Svaars. It was, of course, in Fritz Svaars' room at 59 Grove Street that Gardstein had actually breathed his last. Although no mention had been made of him by Perelman, the police very much hoped that Peter the Painter would also be hiding out in Sidney Street. It was decided that it would be foolish to take any action in the dark, there being too great a chance that the men might escape.

The next day, the police took every possible action to give themselves the advantage in what might very well turn into a gun battle. It was known that the men holed up in Sidney Street were armed and nobody wished for a repeat of the Houndsditch massacre. So throughout the day on 2 January, armed police moved surreptitiously into Sidney Street and the surrounding area. The first action that they took was to evacuate the house. It was split up into a number of flats, all occupied by foreign Jews. It took a good deal of doing, because the other occupants of the house included families with babies and also a querulous 90-year-old man. All the time that this was going on, the police were keenly aware that in rooms above them were desperate armed men who had killed before and had absolutely nothing to lose.

By the time that 100 Sidney Street had been cleared of everybody except the suspects, it was growing dark. The decision was made to postpone the arrests again until the following morning. The house was by this time surrounded by armed police who were hidden on rooftops and in doorways. Anybody attempting to leave the place would be spotted at once and so there was little chance of their quarry escaping.

A word should be said at this point about the firearms being used by the two parties in both the Houndsditch murders and what was later to become known as the Siege of Sidney Street. In recent years, concern has frequently been expressed at the sophisticated weaponry used by foreign and ethnic minority gangsters in this country. It is claimed, for instance, that some 'Yardy' gangs use automatic weapons such as sub-machine guns. Calls have been made for police firearms to be upgraded to reflect this new threat. This is not a new idea.

At the time of the Tottenham Outrage, Houndsditch murders and Siege of Sidney Street the police were armed with an assortment of old and fairly ineffective weapons. The official pistol, still at that time issued to constables on night duty in the outer suburbs, was the Webley .45 revolver. At Sidney Street, a variety of other firearms were brought into action, including shotguns and .22 rifles from a shooting range. These very low-powered rifles were the same calibre as and little more powerful than airguns. Until a few years ago they were commonly seen in fairground shooting galleries. None of these weapons was accurate over more than a few yards.

By contrast, the professional revolutionaries who were holed up in the house at Sidney Street had brand new Mauser semi-automatic pistols. These were the state of the art in firearms at that time. The Mauser could, with the addition of a wooden stock, be converted into a carbine. They were sighted to and accurate at a thousand yards. These were modern, military weapons and, as soon became obvious, it was hopeless expecting the police to be able to match such firepower.

At first light on the morning of 3 January, a cold morning with occasional flurries of sleet and snow, two men walked up to the front door of 100 Sidney Street. Considering the meticulous plans which had been made to avoid any casualties, this seems in retrospect to have been a most foolhardy action, almost guaranteed to end in tragedy. Inspector Wensley and Sergeant Leeson led a small body of police to the house and then rapped sharply on the front door. There was no reply. A handful of gravel was scooped up from the road and thrown up at the windows in the upper storeys. Whereupon all hell broke loose.

One of the upstairs windows was smashed and through the broken pane a hail of fire was directed on to the police officers below. For a moment it looked as though, despite all their careful preparations, the Houndsditch massacre was about to be repeated on a larger scale. By a miracle, only one officer was actually wounded. Sergeant Leeson had been struck in the chest and ankle. He was carried to safety. In a moment of bathos, he declared, 'I'm dying! Bury me at Putney.'

The police returned fire at once, but it was obvious from the start that it was an unequal exchange. The trapped men were firing coolly at anybody who came into sight. The police shot back with their assorted old revolvers, shotguns and fairground rifles, but they were no match for the military weapons being used by the snipers holed up in 100 Sidney Street. The men there moved from front to rear of the house, maintaining a withering fire.

This was the beginning of what became known as the Battle of Stepney or the Siege of Sidney Street. With over 200 police in the immediate vicinity of Sidney Street, many of them armed, and only two men on the other side, it might have looked initially to be a hopelessly unequal contest. So it was, but the disadvantage was all on the side of the police. They fired dozens of shots towards 100 Sidney Street, but to little effect. The police tried various ways to distract the men, with a view to storming the house. At one point, a tailor's dummy was dressed as a policeman and held up in the window of a house opposite No 100. It was quickly riddled with bullets. The hope had been that if fire could be drawn in this way, then perhaps the gunmen would run out of ammunition. As the morning drew on, though, it became plain that the two terrorists had an apparently inexhaustible supply of ammunition for their weapons.

A large crowd had gathered at either end of Sidney Street and many of the thousand or so police officers who were now on the scene were occupied more with keeping back curious spectators. There were two reasons

for this. Apart from the natural desire of the police to avoid any further casualties, there was a fear that if the crowds of local residents, most of whom
were of foreign extraction, were allowed to surge forward in the direction
of the shooting, then the two trapped men might be able to slip out of the
house and lose themselves among the innocent sightseers.

Three hours passed in this fashion. Newspaper reporters arrived and took
up position on the roof of the Rising Sun public house. A newsreel team
from the Pathe News also set up a camera to record the exciting events for
the entertainment of cinema audiences. It was gradually becoming crystal
clear that the police had not the least idea of what they were going to do
next. There had been a handful of casualties, including a cat and a dog.
Some of the neighbours insisted on ignoring police warnings and returned
to their homes. The postman made his usual morning delivery, seemingly
unworried by the gun battle raging around him.

At about 10 a.m., the decision was reluctantly made to call for military
assistance. The closest army base was the Tower of London, where the Scots
Guards were stationed, and a message was dispatched there for the aid of
some marksmen. At the same time, a senior officer contacted the Home
Secretary, Winston Churchill, in order to secure his permission for the
move. Churchill was in the bath when the telephone rang, but answered it
anyway. He at once gave his consent to military intervention and then took
a most unusual step. He decided to visit the scene of the fighting himself.
He was later criticised by the Conservative opposition for this move. As he
later wrote himself:

> In these circumstances, I thought it my duty to see what was going on myself,
> and my advisers concurred in the propriety of such a step. I must, however,
> admit that convictions of duty were supported by a strong sense of curiosity
> which perhaps it would have been well to keep in check.

Churchill got there at about half past eleven, just as troops from the 1st
Battalion Scots Guards, who had arrived a few minutes earlier, were preparing for action. Some had newspaper boards lain in the road, on which
they lay comfortably and began trading shots with the snipers in the nearby
house. Another group of soldiers took up position on the roof of a brewery
which overlooked the back of 100 Sidney Street. From this vantage point
they were able to see right into the room at the back of the house and their
presence confined Sokoloff and Svaars to the front rooms.

The arrival of the soldiers was greeted with cheers and cries of 'Hurrah for England'. Churchill, when he stepped from his car, was taunted with shouts of, 'Who let them in?' This was a clear reference to the perceived shortcomings of the Liberal government's policy on immigration. The shooting continued with the troops managing to keep the two cornered terrorists from coming to close to their windows to fire. It was at this point that the Home Secretary's position began to look a little odd. The police and soldiers present all seemed to assume that as Home Secretary Churchill was in some sense about to take command. In fact, nothing was further from his mind. As he later wrote: 'I saw now that I should have done better to have remained quietly in my office. On the other hand, it was impossible to get into one's car and drive away while matters stood in such great uncertainty, and moreover were extremely interesting.'

He stood next to a press photographer, peering cautiously round the corner as the bullets whistled overhead. As Arthur Balfour, the former prime minister, later remarked in the House of Commons: 'We are concerned to observe photographs in the illustrated newspapers of the Home Secretary in the danger zone. He and the photographer were both risking valuable lives. I understand what the photographer was doing, but what was the Right Honourable gentleman doing?'

Churchill himself years later called Balfour's comments 'Not altogether unjust'. Nevertheless, being on the scene in this way, Churchill felt that the least he could do was to offer some practical advice. He had, after all, a military background. The main thing that he thought would help would be to bring in some more specialised army units than the Scots Guards. Members of the Royal Engineers were summoned by telephone from Chatham. Churchill also thought that if nothing else would do the trick, then it was worth shelling the building. This later seemed to most people to have been a grotesque overreaction to the problem of two men hiding in a London house. He also suggested that the house might perhaps be stormed if the attacking forces could shelter behind large sheets of steel. It was an interesting idea and police officers were dispatched to the Whitechapel bell foundry to see if they had anything of the sort on their premises.

As it happened, neither the sappers nor the artillery were needed. At about two in the afternoon, smoke was seen to be coming from the upstairs windows at 100 Sidney Street. The fire brigade was summoned, but when they arrived Churchill refused them permission to tackle the fire. It was, he felt, too dangerous. The firing had stopped by now and smoke and flames were pouring from the windows of the besieged house. It was never established whether or not the fire had been caused by stray bullets or if the two men had decided to torch the house before shooting themselves, thus going out in a blaze of glory.

By the time the horse artillery which the Home Secretary had authorised came galloping up, the house was all but gutted and the battle was over. Eventually, the fire brigade were allowed, under a heavily armed guard, to approach the fire. No 100 Sidney Street had been destroyed. The corpses of two men were recovered from the charred ruin and they were conclusively identified as being William Sokoloff and Fritz Svaars. Of the supposed mastermind of the terrorist gang, Peter the Painter, there was no sign, either then or later. If he had ever existed, he had vanished forever.

Many years later, the theory was advanced that Peter the Painter, the supposed agent provocateur at the back of the Houndsditch murders, had been somehow warned by the police before the house in Sidney Street was surrounded and had been allowed to slip away and leave the country under police protection. This idea is frankly absurd. Of all types of criminal, none is hated more by the police than the man who shoots down unarmed officers. They will pursue such a person to the ends of the earth and wait for years if need be to bring him to justice.

Consider the case of Liam Quinn who, in February 1975, shot dead PC Stephen Tibble, an unarmed policeman. Quinn fled to Ireland where he served time in prison for an assault. After his release, he returned to America, for he had US citizenship. The British police pursued him to San Francisco and instigated extradition proceedings. Finally, thirteen years after the death of PC Tibble, he was flown back to this country to stand trial. This is an example of the dogged determination shown by the police when they wish to bring to justice somebody responsible for killing one of their own. They never give up, even after many years.

The notion that less than a month after the shooting dead of three unarmed colleagues, the Metropolitan Police would be bowing to the demands of political expediency to allow one of the members of the gang which carried out the murders to escape scot-free is absolutely incredible. The presence of the Home Secretary at the scene of the siege has been cited as evidence in support of this scenario. By this reckoning, Churchill's purpose in being on the corner of Sidney Street was part of a wider game of diplomacy with Russia.

The Battle of Stepney passed into London folklore, with thousands of families preserving traditions about relatives who had been involved in the affair in one capacity or another. The East End has certainly never seen anything like it before or since. In September 2008, Tower Hamlets Council made the strange decision to commemorate the Houndsditch murders and the Siege of Sidney Street by naming two new blocks of council flats Peter House and Painter House. This provoked anger from the Metropolitan Police, who were unable to see why such a man should be celebrated in this way. Even today, there is no certainty as to whether or not Peter the Painter really existed. Various Latvian revolutionaries have been identified with him, but none convincingly. The Mauser pistols used during the Siege of Sidney Street were colloquially referred to as 'Peter the Painters' for a couple of decades after the affair. This was especially the case during the Irish Civil War in the early 1920s. It was thought to be a way of celebrating the memory of a man who had supposedly been responsible for the deaths of three British police officers; something which many Irishmen at that time felt to be no bad thing.

The shootings in Tottenham, Houndsditch and Stepney did not do a great deal for the peaceful relations in this country between Jew and gentile. Fears about immigration were already running high and the notion that a new labour force from Eastern Europe was creating unemployment among the British was becoming common. Anti-Semitism was on the increase throughout the whole country. In Wales that year, this took the form of the first anti-Jewish riots in Britain since the Middle Ages.

Tredegar was a mining town in Wales. There was an economic slowdown in 1911 and many of the workers in both the mines and the nearby iron-works were finding it hard to make ends meet. The Jews in the town were mostly traders and shopkeepers, and some owned houses which they rented out. After the pubs closed on 19 August, a group of men decided to attack one of the Jewish shops. Others joined in and the affair turned into an orgy of looting and destruction, with hundreds of men involved. Altogether, eighteen Jewish shops were looted and sacked. The rioting then spread to Ebbw Vale and at that point the police appealed for military assistance, being quite unable to cope.

Elements of the Somerset Light Infantry and the Worcester Regiment were sent to the towns and engaged the rioters. Several bayonet charges were made to clear the streets. Eventually, the disorder subsided, but it was a grim warning of the fragile state of affairs that existed between the

Jewish communities in Britain and the wider society in which they lived. There is no doubt at all that immigration, and in particular Jewish immigration, was a matter of great concern to the ordinary man and woman in the street. A look at some of the newspaper editorials after the so-called Battle of Stepney gives us an idea of how people were feeling about immigration and its supposed connection with crime in general and terrorism in particular. In January 1911, a few weeks after the Houndsditch murders and the Siege of Sidney Street, the *East London Observer* had this to say about the Whitechapel area: 'It is doubtful if there is more than a score of English families living within a radius of 500 yards of Sidney Street. Certainly there is not a single English tradesman there; the public houses are tenanted by Jews and foreigners, and foreign drinks are almost solely consumed.'

A neater description of the 'separate communities', about which many people today are worried, would be hard to find. Substitute 'Jew' for 'Muslim' in this piece and it could be reprinted tomorrow. *The Times* was, as one would expect, a little more measured in its analysis of the situation. Their conclusion, though, was quite the same: foreigners were to blame for a lot of violent crime. Even before the affair at Sidney Street, an editorial published after the Houndsditch police murders was blunt about the matter:

> Now the British criminal never does a thing like that. Burglars very rarely use firearms at all. A savage delight in the taking of life is the mark of the modern Anarchist criminal. We have our own ruffians, but we do not breed that type here and we do not want them.

In the next chapter, we shall look at the murder of Leon Beron, a crime which may well have been connected with the events in Stepney. Following the discovery of Beron's corpse on Clapham Common on New Year's Day 1911, the *South-Western Star* was indignant. An editorial made their views plain: 'Why should people who have murders to do invade a select neighbourhood like Clapham? Above all, why should alien Jews come here? We sincerely hope that neither Clapham nor Battersea is about to be overrun by undesirables as other parts of London have been.'

Even the king expressed his concerns about the connection between immigration and terrorism. He told the then Home Secretary, Winston Churchill, that he hoped that 'These outrages by foreigners will lead you to consider whether the Aliens Act could not be amended so as to prevent

London from being infested by men and women whose presence would not be tolerated in any other country'.

This, of course, touched upon a point that we have seen many times before, the notion that Britain was a soft touch for dangerous foreigners who felt that they could settle here and carry on in a way that other countries simply would not put up with. Due to Britain's reputation for allowing all those who were fleeing from tougher and more law-abiding regimes to enter the country and the pressure they were under to tighten their immigration laws, there was in Europe barely concealed glee at what had happened at Houndsditch and Sidney Street. The Berlin *Lokalenzeiger* summed up the case by remarking, 'We organise such matters better in Germany'.

8

THREE TRIALS

One of the recurring features seen in recent years is the constant efforts of successive governments to crack down on both immigration and terrorism, only to see their new laws and initiatives overturned by the courts. Readers will probably recollect many examples of this happening. Convicted foreign criminals facing deportation seek a judicial review and are then given indefinite leave to remain in this country. Terrorists cannot be detained because it infringes their human rights. Preachers of hatred are left at liberty because to send them back to their own country would put them at risk.

Most of us tend rather to assume that problems of this kind are a sign of the times or the mark of a judiciary more concerned about the rights of terrorists and foreign criminals than they are about the interests of the ordinary, law-abiding majority. Once more, we shall see that such feelings are not at all new and have in fact also been a part of life in this country for over a century.

The four people who had been charged in connection with the raid on the Houndsditch jeweller's and the subsequent murder of the three police officers appeared for trial at the Old Bailey on 25 April 1911, a little under four months after the Battle of Stepney. It seemed to everybody that the police had done their job well and that here in the dock stood those responsible for the Houndsditch murders.

Zurka Dubof and Jacob Peters were charged with the murder of Sergeant Tucker and they and the other two, John Rosen and Nina Vassileva, were charged with conspiring to rob Henry Samuel Harris of his property. Nina Vassileva was also charged with being an accessory after the murder. It seemed to be an open-and-shut case.

Evidence was first given by the police of the events of that dreadful night. None of this was disputed by the defence. The surviving officers who had been in Cutler Street during the shooting testified that they had viewed George Gardstein's corpse in the mortuary and that there was not the least doubt that this was one of the men who had rushed out of 11 Exchange Buildings firing at them. None of this implicated the men and woman in the dock, of course. They had certainly been associated with the dead man, but that was a long way from showing that they had had any part in an attempted robbery, let alone the murder of three policemen.

The next witness was, at least to begin with, more damaging to the defendants. Isaac Levy had been on his way home from Liverpool Street station when he heard the sound of shooting. He was walking along Arrow Alley, when he saw three men walking towards him. A woman was also in the party and walking a little behind the others. Two of the men were apparently holding up the third, whom Mr Levy thought was drunk. As they approached him though, the two men brandished pistols at him and warned him not to follow them. He then reached Cutler Street and saw four policemen lying on the ground at the entrance to Exchange Buildings. He at once made his way to Bishopsgate police station and told them that some of their officers had been hurt and that they needed to send an ambulance.

Once again, this evidence was accepted by both prosecution and defence. Now came the bombshell. Isaac Levy had picked out Dubof, Peters and Vassileva from identity parades. He had positively identified them as the group he had seen carrying George Gardstein away from the scene of the shooting. He had also seen Gardstein's corpse and identified him as the third man, the one who had appeared to be drunk. If Levy's evidence stood, it was deadly to three of those in the dock and would be enough to hang two of them.

J.B. Melville, the defence counsel for Peters and Dubof, rose to cross-examine this star witness for the Crown. The story that he pieced together from the various other witness statements that had been entered as evidence was rather at odds with what Mr Levy had just told the court. To begin with, when he had reported seeing the four injured police officers after going to Bishopsgate police station, he had made no mention at all of being accosted by armed men. It was only when the police had called round to see him the following day that he had thought this worth mentioning. His explanation in court for this lapse was that his wife was about to give birth and he did not want to be kept too long at the police station. Even more damning, in the statement he gave the next day he told the police categorically that he would not be able to identify the men he had seen again.

In the witness box, he had told the court that he had picked Peters and Dubof out from a line up of fifteen men. It now turned out that only five of the men in the line up were foreigners, the rest looked conspicuously English. There was also confusion about the circumstance in which he had seen and identified Gardstein's body. It was beginning to look to the court as though he had indeed seen the killers escaping, but that the police had encouraged him to identify their suspects and swear a statement to the effect that he recognised them.

There was at that time far more trust in the police and their incorruptibility than is now the case, but even so, this was all looking very dodgy. On 2 May, the judge, Mr Justice Grantham, stepped in. He told the jury that he had listened very carefully to all that had been said and that he could not allow them even to consider a verdict of guilty upon such slender evidence. The police case was falling apart.

Various other witnesses were called, as the charges of conspiracy to rob the jeweller's were still to be dealt with. One of these witnesses was a man we shall be meeting again later in this chapter, Errico Malatesta, a famous anarchist. He testified that he had supplied the cutting torch which was being used in the attempted break-in. More identification evidence was given by the landlord of Exchange Buildings and also by other passers-by who had seen the group of people heading towards Grove Street. It seemed pretty clear that Nina Vassileva had been a friend of George Gardstein and also involved in renting the houses at Exchange Buildings. John Rosen's role in the enterprise was somewhat shadowy.

Halfway through the trial, Mr Justice Grantham made an extraordinary intervention. He told the court that he believed that the all the men involved in the killing of the three policemen were dead. In effect, he was telling the jury that as far as he was concerned, none of the defendants had had anything to do with the business. Thus, the jury's eventual verdict was something of an anticlimax. The three men were acquitted of all charges, and Nina Vassileva was convicted of the conspiracy charge. They added a rider, asking that she not be deported as a result of this conviction. She was sent to prison for two years, with no recommendation for deportation after serving her sentence.

The police believed strongly, both before and after this fiasco, that they had caught the right people. It is entirely possible that they had done so.

What was plain was that they had also massaged the identification evidence in order to make it strong enough to stand up in court. It was this over-egging of the pudding which really dealt the death blow to the case against the men.

Nina Vassileva appealed against her sentence. In July, her appeal was heard at the High Court by the Lord Chief Justice sitting with two other judges. He ruled that there had been no real evidence at all to connect her to the conspiracy to rob the jeweller's shop. It was the fact that she had been George Gardstein's mistress that had implicated her, and she might simply have been present in the house in Exchange Buildings in that capacity, rather than as a member of the gang of robbers. Vassileva was freed at once.

Three of those who stood trial for their parts in the Houndsditch affair faded into obscurity following their acquittal. One however, although acquitted of any part in the shooting of three men, went on to end his career boasting of having shot thousands. Jacob Peters went back to Russia and after the 1917 revolution he became a member of the Soviet secret police, the *Cheka*. He was noted for being a particularly ruthless and cold-blooded operator, even at a time and place well known for unscrupulous and indiscriminate killing. He claimed to have been personally responsible for 6,000 executions. In 1938, he was himself shot during Stalin's great purges. There is a statue of him in Riga, where he is regarded as something of a national hero. It is said that during the Second World War, when Churchill met Stalin and Roosevelt at the summit in Potsdam, Churchill took the opportunity to congratulate Stalin on having had Jacob Peters executed.

What of the legendary Peter the Painter? Some claimed that Jacob Peters was in fact Peter the Painter. Others maintain that there was never such a person at all and that he was invented by some of the anarchists in order to throw the police off the scent of real terrorists.

The police murders of 1909 and 1910, together with the Sidney Street Siege, focused attention on the Jewish community of London's East End and not in a favourable way, either. There had already in the early part of the century been widespread dismay at the large numbers of Eastern European asylum seekers who had been flooding into the country. The 1905 Aliens Act had been designed to address the fears that some in the larger cities had, that their communities were being swamped with foreigners with whom they had little in common. Now they had been vindicated. This was seen as the result of successive government's 'open-door' policies. There were renewed demands for action, both to stem the tide of asylum seekers and also to deport those already here who were convicted of criminal offences. Again, both sentiments are likely to be familiar to the modern-day observer of life in twenty-first-century Britain.

This dissatisfaction with the state of the laws to regulate immigration into this country was not diminished by two other trials which took place in the year following the Houndsditch murder trial. The first of these was that of another Jew, Stinie Morrison. The second was that of the anarchist Errico Malatesta for criminal libel.

As we saw in the previous chapter, the police received the tip-off about the hiding place of the two men wanted in connection with the Houndsditch murders some time on 1 January 1911. At about 8 a.m. on that same day, a policeman patrolling Clapham Common in south London discovered the body of a man lying in some bushes. He had been stabbed to death and his face mutilated. His name was Leon Beron. This was the beginning of the classic murder case, which became known in the press as the Clapham Common Mystery.

Inquiries soon revealed that the dead man had travelled to the area in the company of another man by cab the previous evening. On 6 January, a poster offering a reward for information was being distributed in east London, where Leon Beron had lived and worked. On 8 January, the police arrested their suspect in the murder, 29-year-old Stinie Morrison, a convicted thief and a Jew.

The fact that the arrested man was a Jew was significant for several reasons. In the first place, Leon Beron had also been Jewish. He and Morrison were both members of the same London community, frequenting the same streets and cafes. There was another reason, though, that Stinie Morrison's ethnicity should be of interest to the public at large. In the last two years, the citizens of London had seen some pretty lively activity on the streets of their city. Protracted gun battles, four policemen shot dead and a number of others crippled for life, to say nothing of an apparent upsurge in crime generally. All these things were attributed to Eastern European asylum seekers, the great majority of whom were Jewish. News that the suspect in the sensational Clapham Common Mystery was a Jew did nothing to calm fears of a crime wave fuelled by Jewish immigrants.

By a curious coincidence, the man investigating the murder of Leon Beron was Inspector Frederick Porter Wensley who, it will be recalled, had knocked on the door of 100 Sidney Street on the early morning of 3 January. In fact, it may have been a little more than a coincidence, because the Clapham Common Mystery may well have been linked to the Battle of Stepney which took place forty-eight hours after the discovery of the corpse on Clapham Common.

The dead man had lived in Jubilee Street in Whitechapel. This is of interest because this was the location of the Jubilee Street Anarchist Club, frequented by those involved in both the Houndsditch Murders and the Siege of Sidney Street. Beron, a Russian immigrant, was known locally as 'the Landlord'. His ownership of a few slum properties in the East End was the reason for this nickname. There were also rumours that he might have been an occasional police informant. It will be remembered that it was a former landlord of one of the gunmen at the Battle of Stepney who informed the police of their whereabouts. Once again, the informer crops up in our story.

Stinie Morrison lived in the same district as the participants of the Houndsditch murders and Battle of Stepney. He was, at the time of his arrest, living only a few doors from George Gardstein, the man inadvertently shot dead by his comrades during the attempt to rob the jeweller's shop in Houndsditch. Gardstein, Fritz Svaars, Nina Vassileva and possibly the enigmatic Peter the Painter were all living at No 59 Grove Street, which was a turning off Commercial Road. Stinie Morrison lived in the same street at No 5.

At Stinie Morrison's trial, it emerged that he knew the dead man and had had bloodstains on his shirt the day after the murder. These he accounted for, not very convincingly, by having had a sudden and unexpected nosebleed, which left his shirt with splashes of blood. The suggested motive for the crime was financial. Morrison seemed to have plenty of money and no visible means of support. There seemed to be much confusion about even such basic matters as Morrison's country of birth. He claimed to have been born in Australia and taken to Russia as a baby, but he had made confusing and contradictory claims about this to the Home Office in the past. His current immigration status seemed to be uncertain. That he was a convicted thief was undeniable. At his trial in March 1911, evidence was produced to show that he had travelled with Beron by cab to Clapham Common. The reason for this journey was unknown and Morrison himself called witnesses to prove his alibi, that he was in Whitechapel for the whole of the time that the murder had evidently been committed some miles away on the other side of the River Thames.

During the trial, which was held at the Old Bailey before Mr Justice Darling, the question of the mutilations found on Beron's face was raised.

These were on both cheeks and took the shape of curious elongated 'S' shapes. The marks had been carved into the dead man's face with a knife after his death and their significance was hotly debated. According to the pathologist who conducted the post-mortem, they were very similar in appearance to the 'F' holes found on a violin. The claim was made that these 'S'-shaped marks were to signify that Beron was a police informer or spy. There was a good deal of discussion about various Polish and Russian words for spies and police informers. There is, for instance, in Polish a word, *spiccan*, which is used for a particularly treacherous kind of spy. It has connotations somewhat similar to the American expression 'stool pigeon'.

These mutilations on the face of the foreign-born Jewish murder victim seized the public imagination. Reference was made in newspapers to Arthur Conan Doyle's Sherlock Holmes adventure *The Sign of Four* and also Wilkie Collins' *The Woman in White*. At the inquest into Leon Beron's death Dr Joseph Needham, Divisional Police Surgeon for Balham, stated in evidence: 'The symmetry of the marks on the face is very extraordinary, like two S's, one on each side of the face. They could not have been produced accidentally. No mere coincidence could have produced them.'

The police were not especially pleased with Dr Needham's ideas as expressed at the inquest. They had already decided that this was a simple case of a robbery gone wrong. The day after the inquest, Dr Needham gave an interview to the *Daily Chronicle* in which he reiterated his views of the marks found on the dead man's face. He said, 'I adhere to the statement made before the coroner, a statement based upon the most careful examination and measurement.'

Both before and during the trial of Stinie Morrison, it emerged that cutting, branding or otherwise marking suspected spies or informers in this way was an accepted practice among some of the left-wing political groups in Eastern Europe. This was not the first time that a corpse had turned up with two 'S's cut into the face. Throughout the whole trial, attempts were made to forge a connection between Leon Beron and the Houndsditch murders or Siege of Sidney Street. None was successful. During cross-examination, the dead man's brother, Solomon, was asked about the men who carried out the Houndsditch murders. He said, 'I did not know Fritz Svaars nor "Peter the Painter".' He was also asked about the anarchist club in Jubilee Street, but denied that he had ever visited it. Inspector Wensley was asked about the Houndsditch murders and replied:

The date of the Houndsditch murders was December 16, and from that date we have been trying to find the perpetrators. I am in charge of the case so far as the Metropolitan Police are concerned. Federof and Peters were arrested, I think, on December 22. 'Peter the Painter' has not been arrested. I do not think it is desirable to say whether the police are looking for other persons in connection with the murder. Sidney Street was surrounded on January 2 In consequence of information received by the police. I shut up the Anarchist club in Jubilee Street.

That Sidney Street had been surrounded on 2 January, 'in consequence of information received by the police', was a clear reference to an informer or double agent of some sort being involved. Once again, the defence was trying to suggest that Beron had been murdered by anarchists in revenge for having betrayed their comrades. Since Stinie Morrison was, by general agreement, no more than a common criminal with no political connections at all, this would mean that he was an unlikely suspect for the murder.

Reading the transcript of the trial, it is clear that the events at Houndsditch and Sidney Street were hovering constantly in the background. The police were anxious to play down any such connection and portray the murder of Leon Beron as a simple robbery, but the defence were keen to suggest that there was more to it than met the eye. Anarchism and the Battle of Stepney emerged as the underlying themes of this strange trial.

It was being hinted that perhaps Beron himself had been the one who had betrayed Sokoloff and Svaars to the police. His home was only a few yards from the Jubilee Street Anarchist Club and he could have picked up information by eavesdropping on conversations by the patrons of this establishment. This would provide a far more powerful motive for his murder, by anarchist friends of the men who had died at Sidney Street. Perhaps the double 'S' also stood for Sidney Street?

In the end, the jury preferred to believe the evidence of the various witnesses who placed Morrison in the dead man's company that evening. They brought in a verdict of guilty and Mr Justice Darling passed a sentence of death.

For the general public, this was yet another horrible murder committed by a Jewish asylum seeker. There remained, however, lingering doubts and a sense of uneasiness about the case in the minds of those who were aware of all the facts. So much so that the Home Secretary, Winston Churchill, reprieved Stinie Morrison a few days before his execution was due to take place. Strangely, the condemned man did not seem at all grateful for this. He steadfastly maintained his innocence and spent his time in prison on hunger strikes and petitioned the Home Secretary to allow him to be hanged after all, so wretched was his life in prison. He died in 1921, his health ruined by the hunger strikes he had undertaken.

In recent years, we have seen governments react to perceived fears about terrorism or immigration by intervening with ill-judged comments or, worse still, by introducing new legislation designed to tighten up immigration control or crack down on terrorism. Often, the political decision is made to try to engineer a high-profile case which will demonstrate to the electorate that their leaders are on the ball and in touch with their concerns. For example, in 2006, then Prime Minister Tony Blair described the decision not to deport the Afghans who had hijacked an aeroplane to this country as being 'barmy'. Even where there seems to be an open-and-shut case where a dangerous instigator of terrorism has been caught and convicted in a British court, as in the case of Abu Hamza in recent years, deportation is often blocked on the grounds that the person about to be deported may be subject to torture or even execution if he is forced to leave this country. Abu Hamza, it will be recalled, was convicted of inciting murder and various other offences. The government found themselves unable to remove him from Britain, because he would almost certainly face charges abroad that could carry the death penalty. This was exactly the situation faced by the British Government in 1912.

After all the exciting incidents involving eastern European asylum seekers which took place from 1909 to 1911, the Liberal government was determined to show that they were not a soft touch for foreign immigrants who came to this country and broke the law or became involved in subversive activity. There was a definite need to send out a clear message, not just to the criminals themselves, but also to the voters who were becoming increasingly restless at what they saw as unrestricted immigration into Britain.

The opportunity to show themselves to be tough on immigration and foreign criminals came in 1912. This involved one of the most famous anarchists in Europe, a man who had actually given evidence at the trial of those accused of the Houndsditch murders and whom the police strongly suspected to have been implicated in the robbery which led to the deaths of the three police officers.

Errico Malatesta was Italian by birth, although he had lived in various countries for most of his life. His family were wealthy and eventually he inherited a large fortune. As a young man, he had taken part in various revolutionary activities, including an insurrection in an Italian province where a town was seized by armed insurgents. He had also spent some time in Egypt, after having been refused entry to Syria and Turkey. He arrived in London in 1880 and soon threw himself into subversive activity on behalf of the international anarchist movement. In 1882, he returned to Egypt to join rebels fighting against the British troops who were stationed there to guard the Suez Canal. He also visited South America and various other European countries, attending the International Anarchist Conference, which was held in Amsterdam in 1907. It will, of course, be remembered that he had supplied the oxyacetylene torch that had been used by the Houndsditch murderers. If nothing else, this alone marked him out as a dangerous fanatic who had escaped prosecution so far by the skin of his teeth. He was, in fact, just the sort of disreputable foreign agitator that the government had assured the public that they would crack down upon. The chance came in 1912.

In 1911, there was a minor war between Turkey and Italy for the control of the North African territory of Libya. This was a matter of interest to Malatesta because he was Italian and had also fought in neighbouring Egypt. It was certainly a matter about which he felt very strongly. In London he had an acquaintance or friend called Ennio Belili. He had attended the anarchist conference in Amsterdam with Malatesta's brother, not he claimed as an anarchist himself but as an unbiased observer – a kind of holiday, in fact.

Up until that time Malatesta and Belili had been friends and fellow anarchists according to most of the witnesses called at the subsequent trial. However, they fell out. Belili claimed in court that the reason for this was that Malatesta had lived at his house for a while and that, in early 1911, the police had made frequent visits to the place, asking about the Houndsditch police murders. At any rate, they argued and in revenge Malatesta printed and circulated a pamphlet about Ennio Belili, accusing him of being a police spy and in the pay of the Italian Government. As a consequence, Belili was shunned by the members of the Italian community in London. He brought an action against Malatesta for criminal libel and the case was heard at the Old Bailey before Mr Justice Phillimore on 21 May 1912.

The evidence was contradictory. Malatesta accused Ennio Belili of also writing a pamphlet about him. He claimed that it was true that Belili was a police spy and that this suggestion could not therefore be libellous.

The police took the opportunity to trash Malatesta's character. Inspector Powell stated that:

> Prisoner has been known to the police as an anarchist of a very dangerous type for a great number of years. He has been imprisoned in his own country and has been expelled from France. He has visited Egypt, Spain, France, Portugal, and, I believe, America, in the interests of anarchy, and wherever he went there was a great deal of trouble. He is known as the leader of militant anarchists in this country – in fact, in the world. Many of his former colleagues have passed through this court and had penal servitude for coining. Gardstein, one of the Houndsditch assassins had been using prisoner's workshop, or working with him for 12 months. A tube of oxygen that was used on that occasion was traced to prisoner, who stated that he had sold it to Gardstein.

This was hardly a glowing character reference for the accused man and in the end he was found guilty of criminal libel and sentenced to three months' imprisonment, followed by deportation under the Aliens Act.

There was a certain amount of satisfaction in official circles about the outcome of the trial. It would, it was thought, send out the right message to other terrorist sympathisers that they would be thrown out of Britain if they abused the hospitality of this country. It would also indicate to the general public that the government and judiciary were going to be tough on offences of this sort.

Several problems now presented themselves in quick succession. To begin with, Errico Malatesta was simply too famous for the British to deport him as though he was a common criminal. The whole process looked to any unbiased observer like a piece of politically motivated revenge for such crimes as the Houndsditch murders. Another difficulty was that the press took up the case and protested that to throw a man out of the country in this way for libel was outrageous. A demonstration was held in Trafalgar Square to protest against the planned deportation. There was yet one more obstacle to deporting Malatesta, one which has been an increasingly common sticking point in our own time when the courts try to throw a foreign criminal out of the country when he has finished his sentence.

During his extensive travels and political agitation throughout the world, Errico Malatesta had somehow managed to be sentenced to death on no fewer than three separate occasions. If he was to be expelled from Britain, there was every possibility that he would end up being extradited to another country where he might face execution. This is a very modern dilemma and quite a few foreign-born criminals have avoided deportation from this country in recent years on precisely similar grounds.

There was, of course, no Human Rights Act in 1912, but there was something almost as good: Magna Carta, the oldest human rights act in the entire world, was called into action. Lawyers began preparing a writ of habeas corpus, which they intended to serve on the Home Secretary. It was the last straw and the deportation order was cancelled. Errico Malatesta left Britain of his own accord shortly after being released from prison.

The cases described above are very similar to those which have taken place in this country over the last few years. The police catch a foreign criminal and bring him to court. The jury decide to let him go again. If he is found guilty, the judge fails to order his deportation. Attempts to deport foreign criminals and terrorists are thwarted by the courts on the ground that the person may suffer torture or execution if deported to his own country. The only safe course of action is to allow him to remain here. Then, as now, there were mutterings that the judges seemed to be more concerned about the rights of the criminals than they were about those of the victims.

9

THE INDIA HOUSE

We have so far looked at the activities of Irish terrorists and also anarchists, some of whom were from various European countries. Another group of outsiders during the Edwardian period also dabbled in terrorism. These were Indians who were living in London. Interestingly, they made common cause at times with Irish nationalists, men such as Eamon de Valera. Perhaps on reflection, this was not so strange. Both Indians and Irish felt that they were living under the yoke of a colonial power which was determined by any means necessary to deny their people control over their own countries.

Today, there is unease about the numbers of Eastern Europeans and asylum seekers who are supposedly entering the country in ever-increasing numbers. As we have seen, these fears were present a hundred years ago, but rolled into one; the main problem was perceived to be Eastern European asylum seekers. Another concern that is often talked of now is the number of young Asians from the Indian subcontinent who are living in this country and becoming radicalised by those who dislike the British way of life. Some of these young people have allegedly gone abroad to fight against the British army in faraway countries. This, too, was a problem with which Edwardian society grappled.

During the late Victorian period, a number of students came to this country from the Indian subcontinent. Gandhi, of course, came to London to study law at the Middle temple. There were many others. Public schools, too, had pupils from India who had been sent to England for their education. This phenomenon was reflected in popular literature of the time: one of the fictional character Billy Bunter's best friends was an Indian called Hurree Jamset Ram Singh.

It was quite natural that these students, thousands of miles from their own country, should form clubs and associations where they could meet and exchange ideas. We talk glibly today of how Muslim youths become 'radicalised', but of course, as was remarked above, this is nothing new. Some of the Indian student groups set up in Victorian and Edwardian England, which were ostensibly for social activities and debates, were, in fact, political organisations whose aims were nothing less than the overthrow of the British Raj. Others had avowedly revolutionary aims from the beginning. For example, the Indian Home Rule Society was set up in London in 1905. It was financed by a number of wealthy expatriate Indians and offered scholarships to students in India who wished to come and study in England. Some indication of the nature of this benevolent society may be gleaned from the fact that these scholarships were offered in memory of the Indian victims of the 1857 Sepoy Mutiny and that those who took up such offers had to sign a declaration stating that after graduating they would not take up any post in India with the imperial authorities there.

The headquarters of the Indian Home Rule Society was in a large house at 65 Cromwell Avenue, Highgate, in north London. This property provided accommodation for thirty students and was open only to Indians. From the beginning, there was a certain amount of suspicion regarding the activities carried out by the IHRS operating from the India House. For one thing, it was suspected that they had links with other independence movements in parts of the world where British interests might be threatened; Turkey, Egypt and Ireland, for example. The IHRS had a French branch, the Paris Indian Society, and this had connections with a number of socialist organisations, including some run by exiled revolutionaries from Russia.

Krishna Varma, the founder of the IHRS, also started a magazine called *The Indian Sociologist*, whose aim was to agitate for the end of British rule in India. Valentine Chirol, editor of *The Times*, denounced *The Indian Sociologist* for what he called its 'disloyal sentiments' and urged the prosecution of those who published it. He also described the India House as the headquarters of 'the most dangerous organisation outside India'. Even the king, Edward VII, became drawn into the controversy surrounding the IHRS and the India House. He went so far as to contact John Morley, Secretary of State for India, asking whether it was possible to prevent publication of *The Indian Sociologist*. The police subsequently visited the India House, taking the names of those whom they found staying on the premises. Krishna

Varma took the hint and decamped to Paris, leaving the IHRS in the hands of a new leader, Vinayak Damodar Savarkar.

There is much in the above story that sounds familiar. Radicalised foreign students, the feeling that somehow an organisation is operating here which is working against British interests abroad, shadowy international figures who are fomenting trouble throughout the world. Change 'Hindu students' to 'Muslim students' and much of what was happening with the India House could have come from last week's papers. As it turned out, the government and police were right to be alarmed at the activities taking place at the Victorian mansion in Highgate. There was an awful lot more to the India House, the IHRS and even *The Indian Sociologist* than met the eye.

It did not take Savarkar long to put his stamp upon the India House. Under his control, the peaceful agitation for home rule in India began to take second place to direct action. The India House became a centre for gunrunning and bomb making. There was a large outbuilding at the back of the house, which was turned into a workshop. A printing press was also installed. This churned out seditious leaflets that advocated attacks on white people in India. Bomb-making manuals were also produced. Among the students staying at the India House were a number of young men studying chemistry and they began to experiment in producing explosives. Savarkar was directly involved in the terrorist activity, emerging from the workshop, according to one student who was staying there at the time, with 'telltale yellow stains of picric acid on his hands'.

Except, as we noted above, for the fact that the students taking part in these actions were Hindus rather than Muslims, what is being described is the modern security services' worst nightmare: large numbers of radicalised young Asians manufacturing explosives in a garden shed. The events at the India House mirror precisely just the sort of scenarios that we are apparently facing in this country today. Some of these students also allegedly travelled abroad to other countries, fighting against British forces in places such as Egypt. Shades of the youths from towns like Blackburn who, it is claimed, have gone to Afghanistan to fight British troops in Helmand province.

In addition to explosives, a quantity of firearms was obtained at different times and smuggled to India for use by terrorist groups there. Crates of Browning automatic weapons thus found their way into the hands of those who would not hesitate to use them against British soldiers in Kashmir and the Punjab. Students from the India House joined a rifle range in Tottenham Court Road and practised their marksmanship regularly. Talks were given in meetings at the India House about methods of assassination. A book by Savarkar, *The Indian War of Independence*, was considered so inflammatory that the British Museum library deleted it from its catalogue to prevent Indian students reading it there.

One of the problems that the police faced was that they had very little experience of Indian politics and did not speak any of the languages used by the students. Scotland Yard therefore teamed up with the India Office, the government department in charge of the colonial administration of India. An officer from the Indian police was seconded to Scotland Yard in order to help them make sense of the baffling strands of Indian political thought. Matters were, however, now moving too fast for even an expert like this to keep up with. In 1908, the IHRS managed to engineer the takeover of the London Indian Society, a venerable and respectable organisation which had been started in 1865 by Indians living in London. They did this by the simple expedient of packing the annual general meeting with their members, thus seizing control.

There were still those at Scotland Yard and in the government who thought that the IHRS were little more than misguided idealists; talkers and intellectuals who posed no threat to anybody. They were proved terribly wrong in the summer of 1909.

Madan Lal Dhingra was a 22-year-old engineering student who was studying at University College London. He came from a prosperous, pro-British family in the Punjab, a family that had disowned him because of his extreme, revolutionary views. As soon as he arrived in England, he made contact with the India House and quickly discovered that he had much in common with the activists who lived and worked there. It was also claimed that he became something of a protégé of Savarkar's. For a couple of years, Dhingra studied engineering during the day and spent his evenings learning about firearms and explosives, as well as becoming more and more radicalised.

On 1 July 1909, a very large event was held at the Institute for Imperial Studies in London. Many Indians, Anglo-Indians and former employees of the Raj gathered for a festival arranged by the Indian National Association. It had been expected that the Secretary of State for India himself, John Morley, would be attending. At the last moment this changed and, instead of Lord Morley, his political aide-de-camp Sir Curzon Wyllie arrived. As he entered the hall, a young man walked up to him and fired a pistol four times into his face. Sir Curzon was killed instantly. One of the guests, a Parsee doctor called Cowasji Lalkaka threw himself at the assassin, trying to wrest the gun out of his hand. There were two more shots and the young doctor also fell dying to the floor.

The killer was Madan Lal Dhingra and he made no attempt to escape, waiting calmly while the police were called before he was taken into custody. After his arrest, things moved very quickly indeed. He appeared in the magistrate's court a week later and a fortnight after that he was in the dock at the Old Bailey. Madan Lal Dhingra refused to allow any counsel to represent him and the trial was over in a day. He was sentenced to death.

Madan Lal Dhingra was hanged at Pentonville Prison on 17 August by Henry Pierrepoint, father of the most famous hangman of the twentieth century, Albert Pierrepoint. Dhingra was a very slightly built young man and Henry Pierrepoint gave him the longest drop he had ever used for an execution. Although he had behaved bravely up until that moment, when the hangman entered the cell Dhingra began shaking uncontrollably and almost fainted on the scaffold.

Dhingra left a statement to be read following his execution. In it he said:

> I believe that a nation held down by foreign bayonets is in a perpetual state of war. Since open battle is rendered impossible to a disarmed race, I attacked by surprise. Since guns were denied to me I drew forth my pistol and fired. Poor in health and intellect, a son like myself has nothing else to offer to the mother but his own blood. And so I have sacrificed the same on her altar. The only lesson required in India at present is to learn how to die, and the only way to teach it is by dying ourselves. My only prayer to God is that I may be re-born of the same mother and I may re-die in the same sacred cause till the cause is successful.

There was a good deal of admiration for Madan Lal Dhingra in other countries which were under British military occupation. The Irish and Egyptian press in particular saluted his courage and dedication to his country's interest.

Events moved swiftly for the India House itself. It did not take Special Branch long to trace the connection between Dhingra and the IHRS. The assassination sent shock waves through the whole British Empire. There had been no assassination of a government official in England since the shooting of Spencer Percival almost a century earlier.

Savarkar judged it prudent to move to Paris for a time. He was promptly arrested on his return in March the following year. The India House itself was raided and the occupants harassed by the police on a more or less regular basis. Some returned to India, while others moved out and concentrated a little more on their studies and a little less on political activity. Within a year or so, the Paris Indian Society had replaced the India House as the hub of Indian nationalist activity in Europe. This was not, however, the end of Indian nationalist activity in this country. When Savarkar returned from Paris, he was arrested and it was planned to deport him. There were still enough members of the IHRS in circulation, though, who wished to prevent this action from being taken. They joined forces with some Fenian activists living in London, including a woman called Maud Gonne. A harebrained scheme was hatched whereby the prison van carrying Savarkar to the port for deportation was to be ambushed and the prisoner rescued. The police, however, were ready for this and sent out an empty decoy van. The whole affair rapidly descended into farce and while the assorted Indians and Irish men and women were breaking open an empty van, Savarkar was already on his way into exile.

This was not the end of Indian extremism. Indeed, things took a most sinister turn a few years later and the Indians became seen, as the Irish were also viewed during both world wars, as a kind of 'fifth column' in England. Not, of course, that the expression 'fifth column' was used at the time; this phrase was only coined during the Spanish Civil War, twenty years later.

In 1911, members of the Paris Indian Society joined forces with Egyptian nationalists in a plan to assassinate Lord Kitchener. This came to nothing, but some of the former members of the India House in London were still determined to fight for Indian independence by means of attacks in Britain. The German secret service, which, even before the outbreak of war in 1914, was anxious to create mischief for the British, had at least some involvement with the Indian nationalists at this time. There were also strong links between the Indians and the Irish republicans. Later on, Italian anarchists became drawn into a plot. After the start of the war with Germany, these activities became known as the Hindu-German conspiracy and its tentacles stretched as far as America. In 1915, a loose alliance of Indian nationalists and Italian anarchists was formed. Their plans included assassinating the British Foreign Secretary, Lord Grey, and also the French President and King Victor Emmanuel III of Italy. The Germans also tried to organise an uprising in India, which would have had the effect of distracting Britain from her war aims on the Western Front.

None of these grand plans came to fruition and by the end of the First World War the Indian nationalist movement in Britain had returned to peaceful means. The twin strains of Indian and Irish nationalism came together for one last time in 1920, in the mutiny of the Connaught Rangers, stationed at that time in the Punjab region of India.

With the exception of a brief and peaceful mutiny which took place at the Curragh in 1914, the Irish regiments of the British army fought as hard and loyally as any other during the First World War, as did the individual Irish soldiers belonging to other regiments. This was in stark contrast to the serious mutinies which took place in the French army during 1917, when upwards of 30,000 soldiers revolted. It was therefore a surprise to everybody when a mutiny broke out in a British regiment in India two years after the war had ended.

The Connaught Rangers had fought bravely throughout the war, suffering particularly heavy losses in the spring offensive of 1918. So heavy were these losses that the regiment was all but wiped out. In 1920, the remnants of the Connaught Rangers, which was an exclusively Irish unit, began hearing frightful stories of the atrocities being committed by the British army in their homeland during the Irish War of Independence. The 1st Battalion of the Rangers, who were stationed at Jalandhar in the Punjab, were especially outraged at what they heard. On 20 June 1920, Private Dawson reported to the guardroom and announced that he was finished with the British army and would refuse to obey any further orders. Instead of having him arrested, the decision was made to treat him as a case of sunstroke and send him to bed for a few days. It was an ingenious attempt to calm the situation, but it failed. Within five days, many more men were reporting to the guardroom and requesting to be arrested, because they were also refusing to obey orders as a consequence of what the British army was doing in Ireland.

This must, at least to begin with, have been the most polite and peaceful mutiny ever seen in any army in the world. When it became apparent that hardly any of the soldiers were now ready to obey orders, the senior officers asked them if they would be prepared then to hand in their arms. Incredibly, the men agreed at once and began collecting rifles and pistols, and taking them to the armoury.

For three days, the Irish flag of green, white and orange flew above the barracks rather than the more familiar red, white and blue. It is curious and perhaps no coincidence that this, the only co-ordinated mutiny in the British army for the last hundred years or so, should have taken place in the heart of the fiercely pro-independence province of the Punjab. The leaders of the mutiny explained to their comrades that they and the Indians shared a common goal: ridding their countries of British forces.

All might have ended without bloodshed, had there not been another detachment of the Connaught Rangers in the hills some miles away. They received a garbled account of the affair at Jalandhar and a rumour was spread that five of the ringleaders of the mutiny there had been executed. There wasn't a word of truth in it, but it was enough to provide the spark. A group of about seventy armed men tried to storm the armoury and seize the weapons stored there. Soldiers who remained loyal to the British opened fire, killing two of the mutineers. These were Privates Sears and Smythe. Without this mad action, it is possible that the high command might have tried to overlook the whole business, but armed conflict between units of the army can hardly be ignored.

Of the 300 or 400 men who joined the mutiny, 88 were arrested and faced courts martial. Some were acquitted and, of those convicted, the majority received sentences of fifteen years' imprisonment. Fourteen were sentenced to death. Of these, thirteen had their sentences commuted to life imprisonment. Only 21-year-old Private James Daly had his sentence confirmed. He has entered the history books as the last British soldier ever to be executed for mutiny. He was shot by a firing squad on the morning of 2 November 1920.

10

THE TERRORISTS OF THE SUFFRAGETTE MOVEMENT

We come now to a terrorist campaign that has almost vanished from British history. Many people are vaguely aware that the Irish planted bombs in London during Victoria's reign, a few might even have heard of the anarchists. Even in books dedicated to the suffragette movement, though, there is almost no mention of the ferocious wave of bombings and arson that was co-ordinated by Emmeline Pankhurst and her daughter Christabel in the years immediately preceding the start of the First World War.

History has been kind to the suffragettes, their popular image being that of martyrs suffering for a noble cause. Perhaps it is because the system against which they struggled was so manifestly unfair that we look favourably upon them and have glossed over the less palatable aspects of their fight. At any rate, we remember now the hunger strikes in Holloway Prison and Emily Davison dying beneath the hooves of the king's horse on Derby Day. That shortly before her death, Emily Davison had detonated a bomb which destroyed part of Lloyd George's home, we have airbrushed from history. The same has happened to the bombs which exploded in Westminster Abbey and other important places of worship, the attempted bombing of the London Underground, St Paul's Cathedral and the Bank of England, and the burning down of many churches.

It is possible that the reason that these actions have been all but forgotten is that they took place in 1913 and 1914, a matter of months before the outbreak of war. The First World War certainly overshadowed a good many other things which were happening around that time.

The fight for the right for women to vote had its roots in the nineteenth century. The extension of the franchise to many working men that followed the 1832 Reform Bill led inevitably to questions being asked as to why it was only for men that this change was being promoted. Why should women too not be allowed to vote? By the turn of the century there were many groups active in promoting this cause. This led in 1897 to the founding of the National Union of Women's Suffrage Societies, whose members became known as suffragists. Progress was being made, although slowly and with many setbacks. Emmeline Pankhurst had been involved in establishing the Women's Franchise League in the 1880s. She was a member of the Independent Labour Party, but had fallen out with them because she felt that they were not treating female enfranchisement as seriously as she wished. In 1903, together with her daughters Christabel and Sylvia, she founded the Women's Social and Political Union (WSPU), whose members became known as suffragettes.

From the beginning, the suffragettes were more militant than previous groups. They favoured direct action of a public nature, rather than quietly working away behind the scenes, as had been the tactic of the suffragists. The suffragist methods had proved sound and looked likely to bring about a change in the law without any intervention from the more strident suffragettes. In 1894, for instance, the law had been changed to allow women to vote in local elections and to stand as councillors.

For the first few years, the suffragettes limited their actions to demonstrations and heckling politicians at public meetings. Following the 1906 general election, though, it was decided by the Pankhursts that this was not enough. Articles began to appear in the suffragette journal *Votes for Women* that called for more militant action. From 1909 onwards there was a tendency towards increasingly violent actions. These ranged from smashing windows in the West End to setting fire to pillar boxes. For the next three years, the suffragettes became more and more aggressive in their actions. In 1910, 116 suffragettes were arrested for various offences. The following year, there were 188 arrests and in 1912, 240.

Once they were in prison, many suffragettes resorted to hunger strikes, another tactic that we have seen adopted by political prisoners in recent years. Nevertheless, the mood of both the government and the ordinary man and woman in the street was hardening against them. On 1 March 1912, a co-ordinated spate of window smashing took place in Regent Street, Piccadilly, Bond Street, Oxford Street and the area around Trafalgar Square. At 4 p.m., while a conference was being held in Scotland Yard to discuss ways of cracking down on the organised vandalism in which the suffragettes were engaged, respectable-looking women all over the West End pulled hammers from their bags and began smashing shop windows. By the time order was restored the main shopping streets looked like a war zone.

The mass arrests that followed these protests clogged up the court system and the prisons, but Asquith's Liberal government showed no signs of backing down. Indeed, with the tide of public opinion now running against the suffragettes, Asquith felt that he could afford to be even more obstinate on the issue of votes for women. It was now that events took a most serious turn and legitimate democratic protest crossed the line and moved from vandalism to terrorism.

In July, Christabel Pankhurst began organising a secret campaign of arson. For some time, there had been attacks on pillar boxes by pouring acid into them and also by the simple expedient of setting them on fire with paraffin-soaked rags. It was now proposed that the houses of politicians opposed to women's suffrage should be blown up or burnt down. This was such a reckless strategy that many prominent supporters cut their links with the WSPU. The Pankhursts had always run their organisation in an autocratic fashion, having no annual general meetings or constitution and publishing no accounts. There was something deliciously ironic about a movement fighting for democratic change which itself eschewed democracy. One woman who fell out with the Pankhursts observed: 'Mrs Pankhurst wants us to have votes, but she does not wish us to have opinions.' This attitude became even more apparent in 1913, when Christabel expelled her own sister, Sylvia, from the WSPU. Sylvia had become involved with a group of working-class women and helped them to set up the East London Suffrage Federation. Christabel told her: 'You have a democratic constitution for your East London Federation; we do not agree with that ... You have your own ideas. We do not want that.'

The year 1913 marked the time when the suffragettes turned to terrorism in a serious way. On 10 January 1913, Emmeline Pankhurst wrote to the members of the WSPU, saying:

Dear Friend,

The Prime Minister has announced that in the week beginning January 20th, the Women's Amendments to the Manhood Suffrage Bill will be discussed and voted upon . The WSPU has always refused to call a truce on the basis of the Prime Minister's promise and has refused to depend upon the Amendments in question.

The government have not told us that they will become law. There are some Suffragists, and possibly some Suffragettes, who hope that an unofficial Amendment may be turned into law. They think that they can stop any militant acts until the fate of the Amendments is known. But every member of the W.S.P.U knows that the defeat of the Amendments will make militancy a moral duty. It will be a political necessity. We must prepare ourselves now. There are different levels of militancy. Some women are able to go further than others. To be militant in some way is a moral obligation. Every woman owes this to her own conscience and self-respect, and to future generations of women.

If any woman does not take part in militant action, she shares in the crime of the Government. I know that the defeat of the Amendments will show thousands of women that militancy is inevitable. Peaceful methods fail. We must prepare for this now. Tell me by letter, or by word of mouth, that you are ready to take part in militancy.

Yours sincerely,

[Signed] E. Pankhurst

The tone of the letter was plain and the implications unmistakeable. Any woman who did not take part in militant activities was as much to blame for the situation as Asquith's government.

The first attack as a result of Pankhurst's appeal was a relatively minor one. On 12 February 1913, the tearooms in Regents Park were damaged by fire. Less than a week later, though, came an action which can hardly be described as anything other than an act of terrorism. At six o'clock in the morning of 18 February, a bomb exploded in a house which Lloyd George, the Chancellor of the Exchequer, was having built at Walton Heath in Surrey. It had been planted by a woman called Emily Davison and several accomplices. Two days later, on the 20th, the refreshments pavilion at Kew Gardens was burned to the ground. There were sporadic attacks on wood yards and empty buildings for the next couple of months.

The day after the attack on Lloyd George's house, Emmeline Pankhurst, who had not known beforehand that the bomb was to be planted, stated publicly that she had incited, advised and conspired with other woman to carry out such actions and that the police need look no further for the culprits. She accepted full responsibility for the explosion. On 25 February, the police arrested her for conspiracy. A few days later, an unexploded bomb was found at Westbourne Park tube station. No responsibility was ever claimed for this, although it was generally assumed to have been planted by the suffragettes.

Buildings were regularly being set on fire throughout the whole country over the next month or so. This was economic terrorism, the aim being to place such an intolerable burden upon insurance companies that they would put pressure on the government to come to terms with those fighting the campaign. The suffragettes were very angry with the established churches in this country, particularly the Church of England. There was no great enthusiasm among churchmen and in some cases downright opposition to the idea of female emancipation. Rightly or wrongly, the suffragettes chose to blame the Church for reinforcing the patriarchal society against which they were fighting. The result was a series of attacks on churches, beginning in April 1913 in Hampstead Garden suburb. This was the start of a wave of arson attacks on places of worship that scandalised the nation and did little to help the cause for which they were carried out. In March 1913, the railway stations at Saunderton and Croxley were destroyed by fire and by early April there had been serious fires at country houses as far apart as Norwich, St Leonard's and Chorley Wood. On 5 April, a racecourse stand was gutted by fire at Ayr in Scotland. Arson was ominous enough, but worse was to come.

The trial of Mrs Pankhurst for inciting the bombing of Lloyd George's house took place on 3 April 1913. She was found guilty and sent to prison for three years.

On the afternoon of 13 April, a few days after the church in Hampstead Garden suburb had been torched, a young street urchin noticed a strange object hanging from the railings outside the Bank of England. It was a milk can and as he examined it smoke began to escape from the top. He called a police officer, who bravely grabbed the can, from which smoke was now billowing, and ran with it to a fountain outside the nearby Royal Exchange. He plunged it into the water, which at once extinguished the fuse.

The bomb, for that is what it was, was sophisticated. It consisted of 1lb of high explosives with a timing mechanism made up of a watch and battery. Had it exploded in the crowded street, opposite the entrance to the stock exchange, it would certainly have caused injuries and probably deaths. There was no claim for responsibility for this device and, although it was widely assumed to be the work of suffragettes, there is an outside chance that it was the work of anarchists. The only real clue was that the device had been attached to the railings in Bartholomew Lane by hair pins.

As attacks continued throughout April, the police came under increasing pressure to put a stop to what was essentially a terrorist campaign. On 1 May, they raided the headquarters of the WSPU in Kingsway and arrested six women. All were charged with conspiracy and brought before Bow Street magistrate's court. Bail was refused and all six were remanded in custody. The case against the women was that they had been co-ordinating the arson and bombings either directly or by giving inflammatory speeches that incited others to acts of violence. The prosecuting counsel announced that anybody who contributed money to the WSPU or printed material for them was likely also to end up in court. It seemed that the authorities were determined to take a very hard line with the spreading violence. The raid on the headquarters of the WSPU had the opposite effect of that which was intended. The violence ratcheted up a notch almost immediately.

On the morning of 7 May, less than a week after the arrest of the suffragette leadership, a man called Harrison was sweeping the choir stalls in St Paul's Cathedral in London. He found a brown paper parcel near the bishop's throne and when he picked it up he discovered that he could hear a ticking sound. It was a time bomb, consisting of a charge of dynamite attached to an ingenious timing mechanism made from a cheap wristwatch and a battery. It had been set to explode at midnight, but the soldering on one of the terminals had broken and so the circuit failed to detonate the device.

This was a significant escalation in the campaign of violence being mounted by the women's suffrage movement. The women evidently had access to explosives and the expertise necessary to turn them into efficient bombs. By great good fortune, many of these devices failed to go off. In May 1913 alone, unexploded bombs were found at half a dozen locations in London, including the National Gallery, Whitehall and the post office in the Strand. Letters bombs were also sent that month; one was found addressed to the chief magistrate at Bow Street court. There could be little doubt in anybody's mind that, if things continued in this way, then it was only a matter of time before somebody was killed. The first death, when it finally came, was not of a member of the public but of one of the bombers herself. The suffragette movement had gained its first martyr.

The Derby was held at Epsom on 4 June 1913. One of the spectators was a 41-year-old woman called Emily Wilding Davison. A graduate of Oxford University, she had been a member of the WSPU since 1906. In February, she had been one of those who planted the bomb in Lloyd George's house and had already spent time in prison for the suffragette cause. She had purchased a return ticket to Epsom that day; something that was to prove of great significance in light of later events.

As the horses came round Tattenham Corner, Emily Davison slipped under the barrier and ran in front of them. She was knocked down by the king's horse, Anmer, and then trampled underfoot by the others. She died four days later and was quickly claimed as a martyr by the suffragettes. It was hinted that she had deliberately sacrificed her life for the cause, allowing herself to be killed to attract attention to the suffragette movement's struggle for the franchise. In fact, the flickering newsreel of the time shows her trying to snatch at Anmer's reins. It looks more as though her intention was to disrupt the race, rather than to be killed. Besides, what suicide would buy a return ticket to the place where she intended to die?

Meanwhile, the attacks on property continued. The day after the Derby, the cricket pavilion at Muswell Hill in north London was burned to the ground. The previous month, a stand at Fulham football ground had been torched. The suffragettes had decided that since sporting events like cricket, football and racing were primarily the preserve of men, they would all be legitimate targets for militant action.

As 1913 drew on, public opinion turned against the suffragettes. The vandalism and terrorism were too much for many to stomach, and support for the movement ebbed away. Even those who had previously been staunch supporters began to distance themselves from the campaign and many people began asking themselves if the authorities were right and that these women were actually a little unbalanced. The attacks on churches did not help matters. In addition to the fires that were being set, places of worship were being daubed with painted slogans and their windows smashed. For some, this was the final straw. By 1914, it was clear that the government had popular backing for adopting a hard line towards the suffragettes.

This loss of support did not affect the appetite for violent action among the militants of the women's suffrage movement. More large houses were burnt, a yacht was destroyed, and many haystacks and timber yards were set on fire. The telegraph lines from London were also cut on more than one occasion. Public opinion might no longer be behind them, but the suffragettes were determined to carry on their campaign of direct action. In the spring of 1914, they turned their attention to art galleries and museums. Paintings were damaged at the National Gallery and glass cases smashed in the British Museum. The response was swift. The National

Gallery, Tate and Wallace collection in London were closed until further notice. Women could only be admitted to the British Museum by ticket. This could be obtained by finding respectable people who would write letters vouching for them and guaranteeing that they would not cause any damage in the museum. Over £1,000 of damage, a huge sum at that time, was caused to the Orchid House at Kew Gardens in February, and in the same month a case containing the Crown Jewels was smashed at the Tower of London.

There was a further escalation when dangerous chemicals and even explosives began to be sent through the post to politicians, including Herbert Asquith, the prime minister. Since Mrs Pankhurst's call to arms in January 1913, pillar boxes had been seen as easy and accessible targets. Acid had been poured into them, as well as bottles of ink and other, even less pleasant, substances. Many had been set on fire by pouring in paraffin or oil and then stuffing a burning rag in afterwards. These attacks were more of a nuisance than a danger. Even so, the nuisance was considerable. Between June 1913 and April 1914, 500 post boxes in the London area were attacked in this way with chemicals or explosives. Over a hundred were completely destroyed.

In 1914, letter bombs began to be sent. This was the first time that this terrorist weapon had ever been used and it marked the beginning of the present practice whereby the mail of politicians is routinely screened for suspicious packages. Most of these letter bombs were crude devices, little more than glorified fireworks with primitive fuses made from matches. The intention was clear though: to injure the recipient. Another tactic was adopted: the sending of containers of sulphuric acid through the post to those thought to be opposed to the extension of the franchise to women. A package addressed to the prime minister broke open at a sorting office, injuring four members of staff when they were splashed with acid. A postman in Fulham was off work for a fortnight with acid burns as a result of another incident.

The terrorism now reached a crescendo of violence, with bomb explosions in London churches taking place every month from March 1914 onwards. In March, a bomb exploded in the church of St John the Evangelist in Westminster. It was a crude device, consisting of a can of gunpowder, which was detonated by means of a candle. Fortunately, it caused only minor damage, burning a pew. Nevertheless, it was a disturbing development. At about half past ten in the evening of 5 April, passers-by in Trafalgar Square were alarmed to hear a loud explosion, which was followed by a shower of broken glass on the pavement as the windows were blown out of the ancient church of St Martin-in-the-Fields. A time bomb, planted during the evening service, had gone off. Smoke poured from the broken windows and the police and fire brigade were soon on the scene.

Two pews were burning in the church, windows and light fittings had been smashed and the ceiling was damaged. Suffragette literature was found nearby. Worshippers that evening recalled that the pew where the bomb exploded had been occupied by a fashionably dressed young woman with a large muff. It was assumed that she had carried the bomb into the church concealed in the muff.

It was fairly plain to the police that if bombs of this type were planted regularly, then it was only a matter of time before somebody was killed by one. On the afternoon of Sunday 10 May, the Metropolitan Tabernacle, a large church near the Elephant and Castle in south London, was hit by the bombers. A fairly large device exploded in the gallery, causing considerable structural damage. A charred note was found nearby, which read: 'Put your religion into practice, and see that women obtain their freedom.' There were no other clues.

There were inevitable demands that the government 'do something' about the bombing campaign being waged in the capital. Combined with the other attacks by suffragettes, such as the cutting of telephone lines and the disruptions to the postal service, there was a definite air of emergency. On the afternoon of 11 June 1914, the matter was being debated in the Commons. The Home Secretary, Reginald McKenna, stood up at about a quarter to six to deliver a reassuring statement to the House that the measures being taken against militant suffragettes were having an effect. He called upon everybody to have patience and trust that the government knew what they were doing. One of his announcements was met with general approval. He said that it was intended to take both civil and criminal proceedings against those who were financing the WSPU. He was five minutes into his speech when the sound of an explosion was clearly heard.

In nearby Westminster Abbey, parties of tourists were making their way to their exits, because it was closing for the evening. As people were trickling out into the sunshine, a terrific explosion echoed through the abbey. A bomb had gone off near to the coronation chair. It had been packed with iron nuts and bolts and so designed to cause as much damage as possible. In the event, some of the stonework on an altar was damaged and parts of the coronation chair were blown off. Although nobody knew it at the time, the

Stone of Scone, the ancient block of stone above which all British monarchs sit during their coronation, had also been broken in half by the blast. This only came to light almost forty years later, when some Scottish nationalist students 'kidnapped' the stone from the abbey on Christmas Day 1950. As they removed it from beneath the coronation chair, it became apparent that the great block of red sandstone was in two pieces.

This attack on the most important church in the country caused an outcry. Three days later, the bombers struck again. This time, their target was another fashionable West End church, St George's at Hanover Square. The explosion occurred during the night and there were no injuries. A very famous stained glass window was however destroyed. Former American president Theodore Roosevelt was visiting England at the time and had a special interest in the bomb at St George's; this was the church where he had been married in 1886.

The following month saw the last of the bomb attacks. On 12 July, another attempt was made to plant a bomb in the church of St John the Evangelist, which had already been damaged in an explosion that March. This time the woman planting the bomb was caught red-handed. She was Annie Bell, a prominent militant. She was caught because the timing mechanism for this bomb was simply a burning candle. The glow had been seen as she lit the candle and the police were sent for. On the same day a railway station near Leicester was burned down and an explosion occurred on a mail train from Blackpool to Manchester.

Events in the wider world were to bring an abrupt end to the suffragette campaign of violence. On 28 June 1914, the Arch Duke Franz Ferdinand was assassinated in Sarajevo. The European powers began preparing for war. By mid-July, when the second attack on St John the Evangelist took place, mobilisation was in hand across the Continent. This led, on 4 August, to Britain's declaration of war against Germany. The First World War had begun.

With the outbreak of war, the suffragettes abandoned their fight and threw themselves into helping their country win the war. It was the sight of women working in munitions factories and taking the place of men in vital services, thus freeing up manpower from the Western Front, which led directly to the granting of the vote the year that the war ended. There was a curious little coda to the suffragette terrorist campaign. Had it come to fruition, its consequences could have been devastating. It was no less than a plan to assassinate Lloyd George, by that time prime minister of Britain.

Mrs Wheeldon and her daughters Harriet and Winnie had been ferociously dedicated suffragettes. When war was declared, they began to oppose it by sheltering conscientious objectors in their home. They blamed Lloyd George, who had by that time replaced Asquith as prime minister, for prosecuting them with such severity. At some point in late 1916, a plot was supposedly hatched to kill the prime minister. Mrs Wheeldon's son-in-law George was a chemist and he supplied Mrs Wheeldon and her daughters with a deadly poison. It was later alleged that the scheme was to ambush the prime minister as he played golf near his home in Walton Heath, the same house bombed by the suffragettes a couple of years earlier, and use a blowpipe to deliver a lethal dose of toxin to him.

Unfortunately for the conspirators, the habit of sheltering conscientious objectors in the house had already drawn the attention of the police. Once again, we meet our old friend, the agent provocateur or double agent. The security services persuaded a petty criminal called Alexander Gordon to present himself to the Wheeldons as a conscientious objector on the run from the police. He was welcomed into the house and snooped around until he found evidence of the assassination plans. Following his report to his police handlers, mail being delivered to the Wheeldons was intercepted and enough evidence was gathered to make an arrest. Early in 1917, Mrs Wheeldon, her two daughters and her son-in-law all found themselves in the dock at the Old Bailey, charged with conspiracy to murder.

There was no doubt at all that something had been afoot. Four vials containing curare, a deadly South American poison, were found in the house, as well as a good deal of incriminating correspondence. However, two very different explanations were advanced during the trial for the presence of the poisons in Mrs Wheeldon's possession. The police case was that they had been supplied by her son-in-law so that Lloyd George could be assassinated in the way outlined above. The Wheeldons, mother and daughters, had a completely different story. According to them, they were encouraged by Alexander Gordon, the police informer, to plan the escape of a number of conscientious objectors from custody. Many of those who refused to join the army were being held in prisons. By 1917, there were so many prisoners of this kind that the prison system could not cope. Camps were constructed to hold all the conscientious objectors. These camps were guarded by dogs and the Wheeldons claimed that the curare that the police had found was intended to poison the guard dogs so that a mass breakout from the camps could take place.

The jury were not convinced by the ingenious defence and Mrs Wheeldon was convicted and sent to prison for ten years. Her son-in-law, George Mason, received seven years and Winnie got five. The other daughter, Harriet, was acquitted.

The suffragette terrorist attacks have been almost completely forgotten today. There is probably a very simple explanation for this. All the bombings took place in the months leading up to the outbreak of the First World War. They have been overshadowed by the events of that terrible conflict. A very similar thing happened in 1939. That year saw a sustained IRA bombing campaign across the whole of Britain. Since the Second World War began a couple of months later, it is this that we remember rather than the IRA bombs. The Luftwaffe blitz on London was so fierce that everybody forgot about the small explosions in pillar boxes and railway stations that had been such a sensation in the early part of 1939. The IRA bomb in Coventry is a perfect example of this process. Nine days before Britain declared war on Germany, an IRA bomb killed five people in Coventry city centre. This was regarded as a dreadful atrocity. The following year, Coventry was reduced to rubble by German bombers. The trifling death of five people the previous year was soon forgotten.

A WALK THROUGH RADICAL CLERKENWELL

One part of London has for centuries been associated with radical and subversive political ideas. It has been the haunt of left-wing intellectuals and foreign-born agitators since before Victoria came to the throne in 1837. Clerkenwell in north London has been the scene of riots and demonstrations, left-wing journalism and one of the worst terrorist outrages London has ever seen. In this walk, we shall visit the site of the first murder of a police officer during a civil disturbance, the pub where Lenin and Stalin had beer and sandwiches together and see the remains of one of London's most notorious prisons, which was also the site of a devastating bomb explosion during Queen Victoria's reign.

We begin at Chancery Lane tube station on the Central Line. Leave the station and walk up Gray's Inn Road, turning right after a while into Clerkenwell Road. This district was known in the nineteenth century as Little Italy, due to the large number of Italians who settled here. This was where Dickens placed Fagin's Den in *Oliver Twist*. It was natural that anarchists from Italy who came to this country should have made their homes here. Among these were Francis Polti and Guiseppe Farnara, who were convicted of planning to blow up the stock exchange in 1894. Errico Malatesta, another Italian anarchist, also lived in Clerkenwell. On the left is the main Italian church in London, St Peter's, also known as Chiesa Italiana di San Pietro. Its design is based upon the basilica of St Cristogona in Trastevere, in Rome.

Turn left after passing St Peter and walk down Herbal Hill. Running across Herbal Hill at right angles is Ray Street. It was here that Francis Polti was arrested with a bomb in his possession. Continue into Crawford

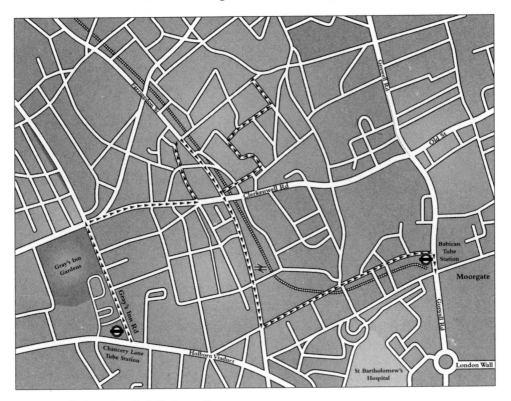

A walk through radical Clerkenwell.

Passage until you come to Coldbath Square. This was once open ground called Cold Bath Fields. It was the scene of a terrible political murder in 1833.

Following the passage of the Great Reform Bill in 1832, many working people did not believe that the law had been changed enough. A meeting was arranged to be held in Cold Bath Fields on 13 May 1833. Lord Melbourne, the Home Secretary, declared that this meeting was unlawful, but there was uneasiness about the legality of this decision. The police themselves were not sure what right they would have to prevent the meeting taking place. On the day, only about 300 protestors turned up and the police tried to disperse them. Some witnesses claimed that the police attacked the crowd. Even *The Times*, no friend of radical politics, said: 'The police furiously attacked the multitude with their staves, felling every person indiscriminately before them; even the females did not escape the blows from their batons – men and boys were lying in every direction weltering in their blood and calling for mercy.' At any rate, there was soon furious fighting, with the police using their truncheons pretty freely.

Some members of the crowd at Cold Bath Fields were carrying knives and in the confusion, three police officers were stabbed. Two of them, Sergeant John Brooks and PC Redwood, were injured, but a third, PC Robert Culley, died of his wounds. The inquest into his death returned a verdict of justifiable homicide against whoever had killed him. The jury that delivered this verdict was cheered through the streets after the inquest, an indication of public feeling at that time towards the police, who were widely seen as agents of a repressive government. The man tried for wounding the other two officers was acquitted at the Old Bailey.

A few years later, in 1848, the Chartists held meetings at Clerkenwell in support of their aim to extend the franchise to all men of whatever class.

The big building facing the site of Cold Bath Fields is Mount Pleasant post office, the main sorting office for the Royal Mail in London. It is where the Cold Bath Bridewell or prison once stood. In 1881, Johann Most, the German anarchist, was sent to prison for sixteen months for glorifying terrorism. He ran a newspaper called *Freiheit* and had gloated over the assassination of the Russian tsar, Alexander II. The whole of his sentence was served in the Cold Bath Bridewell.

Turn right and walk into Farringdon Road. The area around Farringdon has until recently still been a centre for radical journalism and publishing. Both *The Guardian* and the *Morning Star* were based here. Cross the road and walk along Farringdon Road for a hundred yards or so. Turn left when you come to Clerkenwell Green. At the end of the nineteenth century, Lenin was living in this area. He and his wife had a flat at Percy Circus, a little to the north of here. For a while, the revolutionary newspaper *Iskra*, which means 'spark' in Russian, was published in Clerkenwell Green.

On the left, you will see a pub called the Crown. At the time that Lenin was living and working in this area, this pub was called the Crown and Anchor and he used to visit it regularly. When Stalin came to London, he and Lenin had lunch here a number of times. Almost next door is the Marx Memorial Library. This building, which was once a school, is where Lenin worked when he was living in exile in London. It is from an office here that *Iskra* was published.

Walk along Clerkenwell Green for a few yards and then turn left into a narrow street called Clerkenwell Row. This winding little lane will lead you to a high wall enclosing the Hugh Myddleton primary school. It is a good deal taller than most school walls and is actually older than the school which it surrounds. In fact, this is the original prison wall from the Clerkenwell House of Detention, which once stood upon this spot. When the prison was demolished in 1893, it was thought pointless to knock down the wall as well and so it was simply reduced in height a little, but otherwise left intact. If you look at the doorways in this wall, it will be seen that they are surrounded with newer, yellow bricks than those which the original wall is built of.

It was of course in the Clerkenwell House of Detention that the Fenians Casey and Burke were held in 1867. Interestingly, when the prison itself was demolished, many underground cells, passages and storage rooms were left untouched. These were used as air-raid shelters during the Second World War and they are still there beneath the school playground. They were opened to the public briefly in the 1990s. Turn left and follow the line of the old prison wall. When you come to Corporation Row, turn right and continue walking with the wall on your right. Just before you reach Woodbridge Street, a turning on the right, cross the road and then turn and face the old prison wall. You are roughly on the spot where the Clerkenwell explosion took place on 13 December 1867. Behind you was the row of houses which was almost completely destroyed in the blast. Looking to your left, you will see a row of houses beginning at the corner of Woodbridge Street. The top floor of the second house on the right was rented by the bombers. They watched from the window as Michael Barrett lit the fuse that was to cause the worst loss of life in a London terrorist incident until the 7 July attacks of 2005. Behind the wall is the school playground and this is the location of the exercise yard of the Clerkenwell House of Detention.

There was, in living memory, a sad survivor of the Clerkenwell explosion. Until the late 1930s, a very old, blind man used to stand outside Chancery Lane tube station, not far from here. He was a familiar sight to commuters and around his neck was an engraved brass sign which announced that he had as a young child been blinded in the Clerkenwell explosion.

Retrace your steps to Farringdon Road and then turn left. Walk down Farringdon Road until you come to the Smithfield meat market. Turn left into Charterhouse Street and then continue until you come to a road called Aldersgate, which runs at right angles to Charterhouse Street. Turn right and you will find Barbican tube station on your right. This was the site of the first fatality in a terrorist attack on the London Underground. In 1897, this station was called Aldersgate. If you enter the station and go on to the platform, you will find the architecture has changed a little since Victoria's reign. Although the platforms are now open to the sky, there was once a roof containing many glass panels. The iron brackets that supported this roof can be seen on the brick columns on either side of the station. It was a canopy such as those still found in the mainline London stations of Waterloo and Liverpool Street. When the bomb went off in a carriage, on 27 April 1897, the force went largely upwards, shattering the glass in the roof. Many of the injuries were caused by broken glass falling on to the panic-stricken commuters below.

APPENDIX 2

IN THE FOOTSTEPS OF PETER THE PAINTER

The East End of London has changed out of all recognition in the last century or so. It is, however, still possible to trace the events of the Houndsditch police murders and the Battle of Stepney. The streets remain, even if some of the buildings are no longer to be found. We begin our walk at Liverpool Street station. Cross the road from the station and walk south along Bishopsgate. After a short distance, turn left into Houndsditch. Walk along for a hundred yards or so until you come to a turning on the left called Cutler Street. Walk down for a few yards and then stop. Now turn round and face Houndsditch. In 1910, Cutler Street was a dead end; there was no access into Houndsditch. A row of houses stood in Cutler Street called Exchange Buildings and they backed on to the shops which lined Houndsditch. It was in this cul-de-sac that a group of unarmed police officers were gunned down by Latvian terrorists in December 1910. Three of the officers were killed on the spot. The only path to freedom for the escaping robbers lay in running along Cutler Street and they simply shot anybody standing in the way. During the shooting, one of their own comrades was accidentally shot. The rest of the gang carried the wounded man, George Gardstein, back to his flat in Grove Street.

We can retrace their steps by walking up Cutler Street and then turning right and immediately left into Harrow Place. We know that this is the route that they took because in Harrow Place, known at that time as Arrow Alley, they encountered Isaac Levy, who was on his way home from work. He saw a woman and two men holding up a third whom he thought was drunk. The men waved pistols at him and rushed past. They must have then turned right into Middlesex Street, known on Sundays as Petticoat Lane,

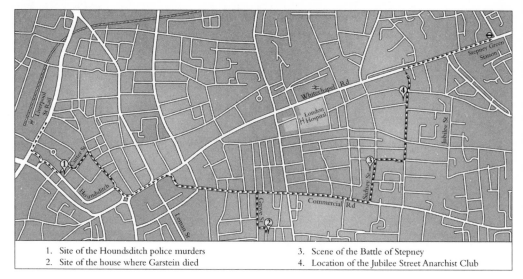

1. Site of the Houndsditch police murders
2. Site of the house where Garstein died
3. Scene of the Battle of Stepney
4. Location of the Jubilee Street Anarchist Club

In the footsteps of Peter the Painter.

and then walked down to Whitechapel High Street. From there, they would have crossed the road and headed down Commercial Road.

Cross over Commercial Road and carry on along it. It is still possible to get a feel for the atmosphere of this part of London. The shop fronts may be new, but if you look up, you can still see many Victorian warehouses and tenement blocks. As you enter Commercial Road, look to the left and you can see some fine examples of how this area once looked. At the time of the Siege of Sidney Street, this district was full of foreigners, mainly Jewish. They have moved further out now, but this is still a district where English is less commonly heard than other languages. A century ago, those languages would have been Russian and Yiddish; today you are more likely to hear Urdu and Bengali.

Half a dozen turnings on the right will bring you to Christian Street. Turn right and then after a few yards, left into Burslem Street. The first turning on the right is Golding Street. This has been renamed; it was once Grove Street. Stop here for a moment and you can recreate mentally the narrow streets which used to be common in east London. Most of this area was either destroyed in the Blitz or rebuilt in the 1950s and 1960s. In this street, at No 59, George Gardstein lived and later died. He was carried back here by his fellow burglars and died a few hours after the murder of the police officers in Houndsditch. It is highly likely that Peter the Painter also lived here. At No 5 lived Stinie Morrison, who was sentenced to death for the murder of Leon Beron, a possible police informer. Although all the original houses have disappeared, Golding Street retains one link with the past. It is still covered in the cobbles which used to be so common a feature of the London street scene. It is rare today to find a street like this. It is very narrow and if we ignore the open land to the left, we can for a moment imagine how it might have looked when the cobbled roadway was flanked by terraced houses, occupied in the main by Eastern European Jews. The front doors opened straight on to the pavement, rather like those we see today in *Coronation Street*.

Retrace your steps to Commercial Road and turn right. Cross the road and continue in the same direction. After you cross the busy New Road, carry on down Commercial Road. A few streets further and you will come to Sidney Street on your left. Many of the old houses have been demolished here or were destroyed by German bombs during the war. The houses where the Siege of Sidney Street took place are no longer standing, but it is still possible to get a flavour of what this street was once like.

Continue up Sidney Street until you get to Sidney Square. The houses on the left are exactly like those where the siege took place. This is what the whole street once looked like. Turn right and walk along Clark Street. The next street on the left is Jubilee Street. It was here that the famous anarchist club was situated and it is also the street where Leon Beron lived. Turn left and walk along for a distance. You will come to a turning on the left called Lindley Street. On the corner of the street, occupied by a modern block of flats and opposite a pillar box, is the site of the old Jubilee Street Anarchist Club. Keep walking a little and on your left are a row of old houses which are typical of how all the streets of Whitechapel and Stepney looked a hundred years ago. On the other side of the road are similar houses, including one with a perfectly preserved Victorian shop front. This section of the East End is like a time capsule.

Keep walking up Jubilee Street and cross the road at the end and walk through Leary square, which will bring you into the Whitechapel Road. It is curious to reflect that this area is now, just as it was a hundred years ago, viewed as a breeding ground for terrorism and radical politics. A little way along Whitechapel Road on the left is the East London Mosque, which has been associated with radical Islam and also linked by some with terrorism. Turning right and crossing the road will take you to Stepney Green tube station.

EPILOGUE

We have in this book looked at terrorism in the years between 1867 and 1914. This period spans the time from the Clerkenwell Outrage to the bombing of Westminster Abbey by the suffragettes. There was nothing special about these particular forty or fifty years; an examination of the last forty years in Britain would show much the same picture. From the anarchist bombings of the Angry Brigade in the early 1970s, which included attacks on the homes of two Cabinet ministers, through the IRA campaign which lasted on and off for a quarter of a century, all the way up to the 7 July bombings and the attack on Glasgow airport; wherever we look in recent British history, there seem to be terrorists at work. The years between the two World Wars also saw a great deal of activity in this field, including in 1939 the most sustained and ferocious terrorist campaign ever mounted against this country. This culminated with the bombing in Coventry in August 1939, which killed five people and for which two Irishmen were later hanged.

Looking back a few centuries further gives us a similar picture. We all learnt at school that the Great Fire of London was nothing more than a tragic accident started in a baker's shop, but that is not what was thought at the time. For many years after the fire, it was believed that the whole thing had resulted from a bomb attack by French terrorists. On 28 September 1666, just three weeks after the Great Fire of London, Robert Hubert, a French Catholic, was tried at the Old Bailey for starting the fire with an incendiary device and hanged at Tyburn. When the Monument was erected a few years later, the inscription at the base referred baldly to 'the most dreadful Burning of this City; begun and carried on by the treachery and malice of the Popish faction'. This part of the inscription was removed in

1830, with Catholic emancipation in the wind, but the fact is that for 150 years after the event, the Great Fire of London was viewed as the result of a terrorist attack.

There is a tendency today to see terrorism as some modern aberration, something that has arisen in recent years and might with luck fade away in time. This is unlikely. Terrorism of different sorts has been a constant backdrop in British history for centuries; it is likely to remain so for centuries to come. The notion that increased vigilance on the part of the public, combined with wise and good laws passed by Parliament, might one day defeat terrorism and usher in a peaceful era, where nobody needs to worry about bombs and assassinations, is a chimera. As long as groups of people in any country feel powerless and aggrieved, some of them will resort to guns and bombs to draw attention to their cause. Terrorist activity in London has been part of the fabric of life in the capital for at least 300 years. We can certainly work to reduce it, but we shall never be rid of it completely.

BIBLIOGRAPHY

Adams, Fran (2003), *Freedom's Cause; Lives of the Suffragettes*, London, Profile Books

Andrew, Christopher (2009), *The Defence of the Realm*, London, Allen Lane

Barker, Felix & Silvester-Carr, Denise, *Crime and Scandal; the Black Plaques Guide to London*, London, Constable

Bloom, Clive (2007), *Terror Within*, Stroud, The History Press

Bunyan, Tony (1976), *The History and Practice of the Political Police in Britain*, London, Julian Friedmann Publishers

Burleigh, Michael (2008), *Blood and Rage*, London, Harperpress

Chesterton, G.K. (1908), *The Man who was Thursday*, London

Connolly, S.J. (ed.) (1998), *The Oxford Companion to Irish History*, Oxford, Oxford University Press

Conrad, Joseph (1907), *The Secret Agent*, London

Davenport, Hugo (2003), *Days that Shook the World*, London, BBC Worldwide

Deacon, Richard (1969), *A History of the Secret Service*, London, Muller

Fawcett, E. Douglas (1893), *Hartman the Anarchist; or the Doom of the Great City*, London, Edward Arnold

Glendon, George (1910), *The Emperor of the Air*, London, Methuen

Glinert, Ed (2005), *East End Chronicles*, London, Penguin Books

—— (2003), *The London Compendium*, London, Penguin Books

Holmes, Colin (1979), *Anti-Semitism in British Society, 1876–1939*, London, Edward Arnold

Kenny, Mary (2009), *The Crown and the Shamrock*, Dublin, New Island

Linnane, Fergus (2003), *London's Underworld*, London, Robson Books

Bibliography

Madden, F.J.M. (2005), *Understand Irish History*, London, Hodder Education

Martin, Fido & Skinner, Keith (1999), *The Official Encyclopaedia of Scotland Yard*, London, Virgin Books

Philips, Melanie (2006), *Londanistan*, London, Gibson Square

Rose, Andrew (1985), *Stinie; Murder on the Common*, London, The Bodley Head

Sweeney, G. (1904), *At Scotland Yard*, London, Grant Richards

Townshend, Charles (2002), *Terrorism*, Oxford, Oxford University Press

Winder, Robert (2004), *Bloody Foreigners*, London, Little Brown

INDEX

Aldersgate tube bombing 35, 36, 145, 146
Aliens Act 1905 38, 67, 87, 89, 90, 113
Allen, William Philip 46–8
Al Qaeda 19, 22, 45, 53, 60, 69
anarchism 20–38
Anderson, Robert 50, 77–9
Angry Brigade, the 150
Asquith, Herbert 132, 133, 137, 140
asylum seekers 20, 86–8, 94, 96

Balfour, Arthur 105
Bank of England, attempt to bomb 134
Barcelona, bomb attack in 25
Barrett, Michael 40, 49, 57–60, 78
Bentley, Sergeant 97, 98, 100
Beshenivsky, Sharon 86
Beron, Leon 108, 114–17
Big Ben 9, 23
Bourdin, Martial 28–30, 34, 81
Brall, Fritz 33
Brett, Sergeant 45, 46
Brighton, IRA bombing of 72

Buchan, John 23
Burton, Henry 69, 70

Callan, Thomas 71–5
Carlton Club, bomb attack on 66
Chester castle, planned attack on 44, 49
Chesterton, G.K. 16, 18
Choat, PC 98, 100
Churchill, Winston 9, 104, 105, 108, 113, 117
Clan na Gael 62, 66, 80
Clapham Common Mystery 114–17
Clerkenwell Outrage 7, 39–60, 64, 76–8, 145
Club Autonomie 28–30
Commonweal 17, 18, 25, 30, 82, 83
Connaught Rangers mutiny 128, 129
Conrad, Joseph 16, 31
Coulon, Auguste 24, 82
Coventry, IRA bombing of 141, 150

Index

Daly, James 129
Davison, Emily 133, 135, 136
Deakin, Joseph 24, 25, 29
Derby, Lord 53–5, 56, 60, 64, 77
Dhingra, Madan Lal 125, 126
Disraeli, Benjamin 53–5, 57, 60, 77
docklands, IRA bombing of 52
double agents, British use of 16, 18,
    24, 30, 50, 72, 73, 75, 76, 79–82,
    140
Dubof, Zurka 99, 110–12
dynamite 14, 28, 31, 63

Engels, Friedrich 49, 56
Explosive Substances Act 1883 65

Farnara, Guiseppe 33, 142
Fawcett, E. Douglas 23
Fenians 30, 39–75, 76–8
Fielding, Colonel William 54, 77

Gallagher, Thomas 65, 70, 79
Gandhi 122
Gardstein, George 99, 111, 115, 148
Gilbert, James George 69, 70
Glendon, George 23
Gonne, Maud 127
Gower Street station, bomb at
    68, 69
Great Fire of London 150, 151
Greenwich Observatory, bomb at
    17, 27–9, 81
Grove Street 99, 115, 148
Guildford pub bombings 72
gunpowder 14

habeus corpus, proposed suspen-
    sion of 54

Harkins, Michael 71–5
Hefeld, Paul 90–4
Henry, Emile 27, 29
Hindu-German conspiracy 127
Houndsditch murders 96–8, 120,
    147, 148
Hubert, Robert 150

India House, the 122–9
Indian Home Rule Society 123–5,
    127
Indian Sociologist, the 123, 124
IRA 7, 52, 62, 63, 69, 72
Irish immigrants in England
    40–3
Irish Republican Brotherhood
    43, 58
Islamic terrorism 8, 18, 22, 42

Jews 22, 23, 87, 88
Joscelyn, Ralph 92, 94
Jubilee Plot, the 70–5
Jubilee Street anarchist club
    115, 149
Justice, Anne 49–52, 57

Kingsley, Charles 41

Larkin, Michael 46–8
Lepidus, Jacob 90–3
letter bombs, suffragette 137
Lloyd George, David 133, 134, 139,
    140
Londanistan 8, 22
London Underground, bombs on
    7, 35–7, 65, 68, 133
London Bridge, bombing of 67

'M' 84
Macdona, J. Cumming MP 26
Malatesta, Errico 15, 112, 114, 118–21, 142
Manchester 'Martyrs', execution of 48
Manchester police murders 45–9
Mansion House, bombs at 63, 64
Marx, Karl 12, 56
Melville, Inspector William 24, 67, 82–4
Metropolitan Tabernacle, bomb at 138
Meunier, Theodule 31, 83
MI5 57, 83, 84
Millen, Francis 71–3, 75
Monument, the 150
Morrison, Stinie 114–18, 149
Most, Johann 12, 15, 18, 19, 83, 144

Narodnaya Volya 13, 61
National Gallery, bomb at 135
Nelson's Column, attempted bombing of 66
New Cross Road, bomb at 34
Nicoll, David 82, 83
nitroglycerine 13, 14, 28, 34, 63
Nobel, Alfred 14, 28
Nolan, Joseph MP 73, 75

O'Brian, Michael 46–8
Ochrana, the 100
O'Sullivan-Burke, Richard 45, 49–52

Paddington station, bomb at 65
Pankhurst, Christabel 130–32
Pankhurst, Emmeline 130–34, 137

Pankhurst, Sylvia 131, 132
Parliament, bombs at 68, 69
Parnell, Charles MP 73, 75
Peters, Jacob 99, 110–13
Peter the Painter 99–101, 106, 107, 113, 115
Polti, Francis 33, 142
Propaganda by the Deed 15, 21

Richards, Rollo 35
Roberts, Harry 100
Rossa, Jeremiah O'Donovan 62
Rossa's Skirmishers 62, 66, 80

St George's church 139
St John the Evangelist church, bombing of 137, 139
St Martin-in-the-Fields church, bombing of 137, 138
St Paul's Cathedral 9, 78, 100, 130, 135
Salisbury, Lord 73
Samuel, Henry 25, 30
Savakar, Vinayak 124, 126
Schnurmann rubber factory 90, 91
Scotland Yard, bombing of 66
secret service, British 56, 57, 77, 78
Sidney Street, Siege of 101–9
Sobrero, Ascanio 13
Sokoloff, William 101, 106, 115
Special Branch 64–7, 78, 79, 81, 84
Stepney, Battle of 101–9
suffragettes 130–41
sulphuric acid 29, 32–4, 65, 80

terrorism, definition of 12
terrorism, theory of 12, 13, 15, 21, 61
The Man who was Thursday 16, 18, 25
The Secret Agent 16–18, 31
Times, The bomb at 65
Tottenham Outrage 86–95
Tower of London, bomb at 68, 69
Tredegar, riot in 107
Tucker, Sergeant 98, 100
Tyler, PC 91, 92, 94, 100

Vaillent, Auguste 26, 27
Varma, Krishna 123, 124
Vassileva, Nina 99, 110–13, 115
Victoria station, bomb at 66

Walsall conspiracy 24, 81
Wells, H.G. 23
Westbourne Park station, bomb at 133
Westminster Abbey 70, 72
Westminster Abbey, bombing of 138, 139
Wyllie, Sir Curzon 125

Other titles published by The History Press

Jack the Ripper: Scotland Yard Investigates
STEWART P. EVANS & DONALD RUMBELOW

£14.99

Join two leading Ripper experts that have joined forces to treat the case of the Ripper's East End murders like a police investigation. Using their unparalleled knowledge of the murders and their professional experience as police officers, they uncover clues about this darkly fascinating case that have remained undetected for over a hundred years.

978-0-7509-4229-4

Victorian CSI
WILLIAM GUY, DAVID FERRIER & WILLIAM SMITH

£12.99

Based on the final edition of William A. Guy's *Principles of Forensic Medicine*, this guide could instruct a detective on the victim's cause of death – or whether they were dead at all. With original woodcuts, case studies and notes on identifying the corpse and walking the crime scene, Victorian CSI will fascinate lovers of crime fiction and of true crime alike.

978-0-7524-5513-6

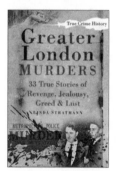

Greater London Murders:
33 True Stories of Revenge, Jealousy, Greed & Lust
LINDA STRATMANN

£14.99

This compendium brings together thirty-three murderous tales – one from each of the capital's boroughs – that not only shocked the City but made headline news across the country. This carefully researched, well-illustrated and enthralling text will appeal to both those interested in the history of Greater London's history and true-crime fans.

978-0-7524-5124-4

The Poisonous Seed: A Frances Doughty Mystery
LINDA STRATMANN

£8.99

When a customer of William Doughty's chemist shop dies of strychnine poisoning after drinking medicine he dispensed, William is blamed, and the family faces ruin. William's daughter, nineteen year old Frances, determines to redeem her ailing father's reputation and save the business. She soon becomes convinced that the death was murder, but unable to convince the police, she turns detective.

978-0-7524-6118-2

Visit our website and discover thousands of other History Press books.

www.thehistorypress.co.uk